Contents

SCIENCE

Contents continued

How to use this book

Scientists, techies, engineers and mathematicians all use journals to keep track of the projects they work on.

Journals are a great space to keep fascinating data from experiments, amazing ideas for new inventions, puzzling questions about why (or how or what or when) along with notes, sketches and doodles.

Project pages

Each project begins with a **question**.
Which is how people have always begun when making something new.

- ★ *How can I make my own fire?*
- ★ *How can I send a funny picture to my best friend... on another planet?*

Challenge units are trickier than the others

There's a **photograph** (to save a thousand words) and some information about the topic; often interesting facts!

To get started on the project, there's a **picture list of things you'll need**. Not everything is listed but all the essentials should be there.

Now comes the fun bit!

1 There are **four steps** to each project. At least, there are four boxes.	**2** Not everything is explained. Sometimes it's because there's not enough space.
3 Sometimes it's because you can tell what comes next from the pictures.	**4** And sometimes, it's so you can work it out for yourself.

On the **journal page**, you'll see lots of different things:

1. Space to write about your project.
2. Space to sketch out your own ideas.
3. Charts to complete with data from your experiments.
4. More step-by-steps to take your project further.
5. Interesting facts and trivia about the subject.
6. Questions to make you think.

Keeping safe

Please remember to keep safe while you are working. You should know not to run with scissors and that hot things (such as a hot glue gun and irons) are well, hot!

But just so you don't forget, there are yellow safety signs on those bits that you need to be careful with; such as scissors and wire and hot glue guns...

Who lives where?

What are the similarities and differences between the world's five main biomes?

A biome is a large community of plants and animals that have adapted to live in a particular environment. The main five biomes are deserts, forests, grasslands, tundras and aquatic.

What you need

five glass jars or containers

natural materials

craft materials

marker pens and labels

1 Label each glass jar with a biome name.

2 Research the main characteristics of the five main biomes (Journal 1).

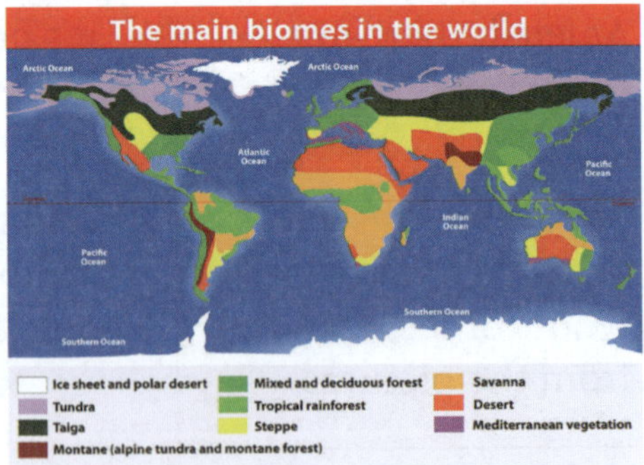

3 Use natural materials to make a miniature biome in each jar.

4 Model a sample plant and animal for each biome.

TARGETING STEM JOURNAL 5 @ PASCAL PRESS ISBN 978-1-925726-10-7

1 Complete this chart of the major characteristics of the five main biomes.

	Deserts	Forests	Grasslands	Tundras	Aquatic
Land or water?					
Hot, warm or cold climate?					
Trees, bushes or grass?					
High, medium or low rainfall?					
Sample plant					
Sample creature					

2 Each of the main biomes is made up of smaller biomes called sub-biomes. For example, aquatic biomes can be freshwater or marine; deserts can be hot and dry, semi-arid, coastal or cold. Choose a main biome and research two of its sub-biomes. Complete the chart below.

My main biome is ______________________________________.

	Sub-biome 1	Sub-biome 2
Climate		
Plant life		
Animal life		
Rainfall		
Special features		

3 The photo shows an enclosed dome at the Eden Project in the UK. Use the photo and the information below to identify the biome they have recreated.

The biome is kept quite hot although they give plants a lot of water in 'winter'. The plant life is mainly scrubby vegetation with a few medium height trees. This biome can be found in southern Australia, Africa and around the Mediterranean Sea.

DID YOU KNOW?

The Eden Project in the UK was set up to demonstrate the importance of plants and to promote the sustainable use of plant resources. In its grounds are two enormous domes with simulated environments including a Tropical Biome covering 1.56ha.

Duck adaptations (1)

Why are duck's feet webbed?

Animals and plants adapt (or change) to survive in their environment. Some adaptations are structural. Structural adaptations are physical features such as having a long bill, feathers or webbed feet.

What you need

pipe cleaners

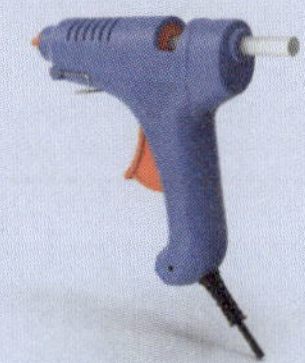
thin flexible plastic or foodwrap

glue gun

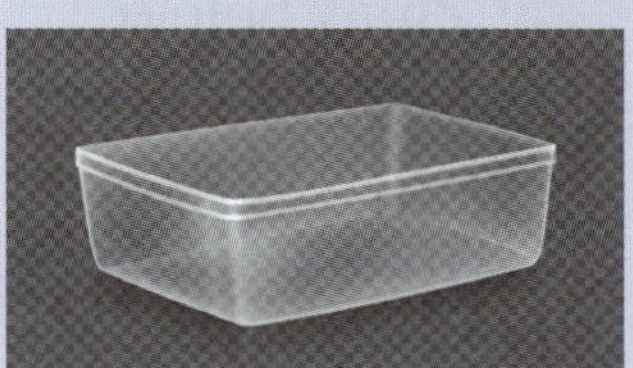
large water trough

1 Make a bird's foot from pipe cleaners.

2 Test the bird's foot in the water trough. Record your results in Journal 1, Column 1.

3 Make a duck's foot from pipe cleaners. Use plastic to create the webbing between the toes.

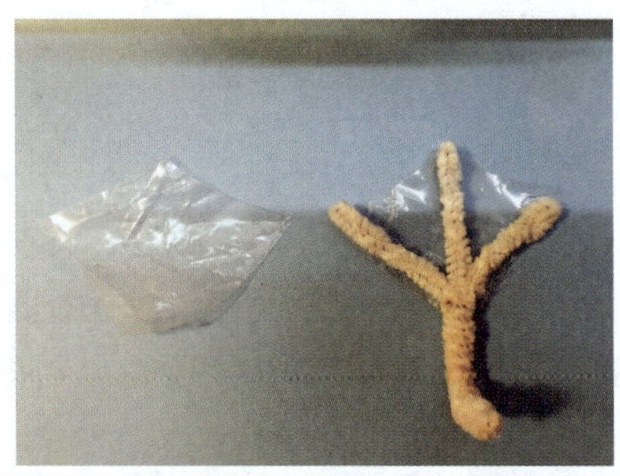

4 Test the duck's foot in the water trough. Record your results in Journal 1, Column 2.

TARGETING STEM JOURNAL 5 @ PASCAL PRESS ISBN 978-1-925726-10-7

1 Complete the table.

Test	Bird Foot	Duck's Foot
1. How much resistance is there to pushing the leg straight down into the water?	☆☆☆	☆☆☆
2. How much water remains on the leg when you remove it from the trough?	☆☆☆	☆☆☆
3. How much resistance is there to pushing the leg across the surface of the water?	☆☆☆	☆☆☆
4. How much water can you flick across the trough using the leg?	☆☆☆	☆☆☆
Other observations of moving the leg through water		

2 How do you think having webbed feet helps a duck? How might webbed feet help a duck take off from water?

____

____

3 Find a video of duck's feet paddling. Observe the spread of its toes as it completes each cycle of paddling. Design a paddle for a canoe or kayak that works in a similar way.

DID YOU KNOW?

Ducks don't have blood vessels in their feet, so they can paddle in very cold water.

TARGETING STEM JOURNAL 5 @ PASCAL PRESS ISBN 978-1-925726-10-7

Duck adaptations (2)

Why do ducks preen?

Behavioural adaptations are ways plants and animals adapt their behaviour to survive in their environment. Dogs hunt in packs, meerkats post sentries when foraging for insects and birds, such as ducks, preen their feathers.

SCIENCE SSU072, SSU073, SSU074, SHE061, SIS065, SIS071

MATHEMATICS MMG084

What you need

petroleum jelly (for example, Vaseline)

thin cardboard

scissors

water

1 Cut two large feathers out of thin card.

2 Lightly rub petroleum jelly over the surface of one feather.

3 Sprinkle the feathers with water droplets. Record your observations in Journal 1.

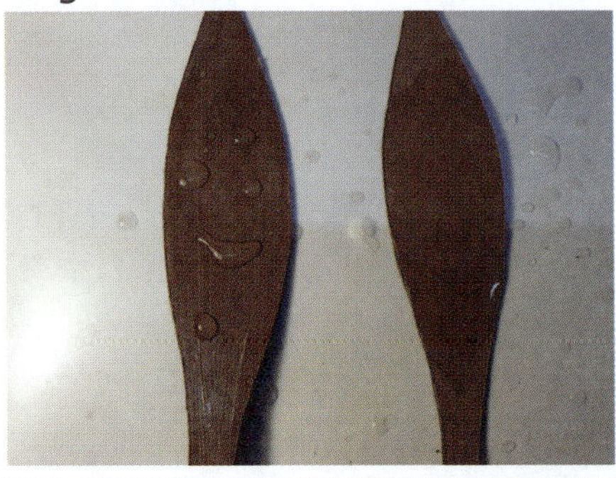

4 Immerse the two feathers in water for a minute. Record your observations in Journal 1.

TARGETING STEM JOURNAL 5 @ PASCAL PRESS ISBN 978-1-925726-10-7

1 Record your observations.

	Uncoated feather	Coated feather
Sprinkling water droplets		
Immersing in water		

How does having a thin coating of petroleum jelly change how cardboard absorbs water?

2 For this task you will need a real feather, a pencil and some hair conditioner.

a. Lightly crumple the feather in your hand.

b. Use the pencil like a bird bill to comb out the crumples.

c. Smooth in some hair conditioner.

d. Now try combing out the crumples.

How does the conditioner help smooth the feather?

3 Birds spread oil onto their feathers during preening. Find out where this oil comes from and other uses it has. Record your research.

4 Detergent is used to clean birds rescued from oil slicks.

a. What else might detergent remove from the bird?

b. What effect would this have?

DID YOU KNOW?

Cleaning and caring for an oil-affected bird can cost $600-$750 and take several months to complete.

4 Duck: Destination South Pole

How could you help a duck adapt to living in Antarctica?

Animals use both structural and behavioural adaptations to survive in their environments. As climates change, animals can die if they are not able to move or adapt to the new conditions.

What you need

modelling materials

drawing materials

1 Complete Journal Step 1.

Adaptation	S	B	This helps penguins to:	Ducks
Webbed feet	✓		Swim underwater	✓
Thick skins				
Layers of fat called blubber under their skin				

2 Complete Journal Step 2 by choosing three adaptations that would help a duck survive better.

Adaptation	I chose this because...
Make nests from stone	There are no reeds or sticks at the south pole

3 Draw or make a model of your duck and its adaptations.

4 Label your duck and its adaptations.

SCIENCE SSU072, SSU073, SSU074, SHE061, SIS065, SIS071

MATHEMATICS MMG084

TARGETING STEM JOURNAL 5 @ PASCAL PRESS ISBN 978-1-925726-10-7

1 Penguins have many adaptations that let them live in a cold environment. In the table below:

a. Tick the adaptations as 'S' (structural) or 'B' (behavioural).

b. Explain how each adaptation helps penguins survive in a cold environment.

c. Tick any adaptations that ducks have as well.

Adaptation	S	B	This helps penguins to:	Ducks
Webbed feet				
Thick skins				
Layers of fat called blubber under their skin				
Huddling together on land				
Dark feathers on their backs				
Preening oil				
Heavy bones				
Nests made from stones				

2 Imagine you are designing a new duck. Choose three penguin adaptations that you will add to your duck. Don't add an adaptation that the duck already has!

Adaptation	I chose this because...

3 How else could you help a duck survive? Write your ideas below or add them to your model duck. Think about how an adaptation could help with:

- Hunting for food ______________________________
- Keeping warm in a cold environment ______________________________
- Keeping safe from predators ______________________________
- Attracting a mate ______________________________

DID YOU KNOW?

More than 60 bird species can be found in Antarctica, including the yellow-billed pintail, a species of duck.

TARGETING STEM JOURNAL 5 @ PASCAL PRESS ISBN 978-1-925726-10-7

Possum magic

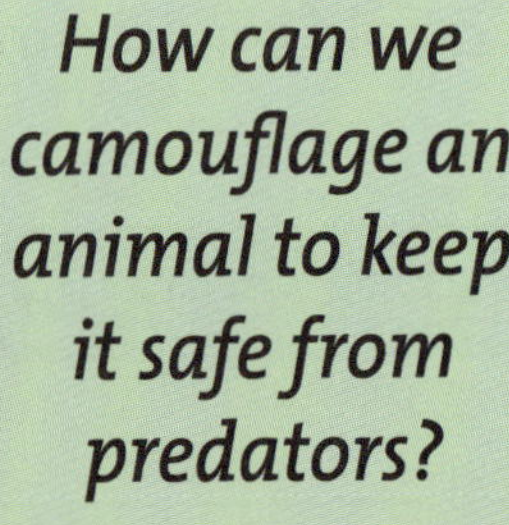

Animals often have predators (including humans) looking for them. Adaptations that help them blend into the local environment can keep them safe from hungry eyes.

SSU072, SSU073, SSU072, SIS071

SCIENCE MATHEMATICS

What you need

thin card

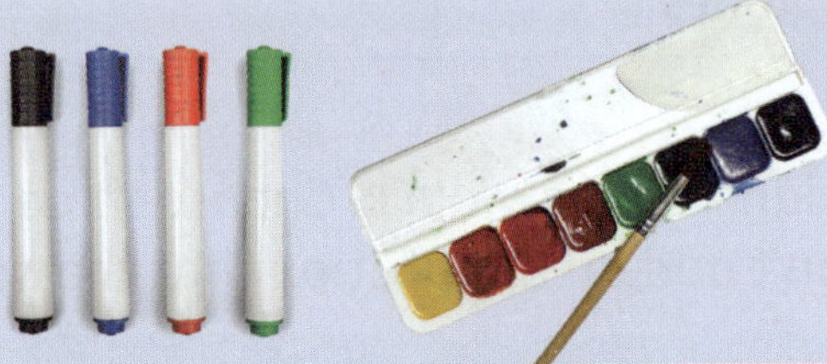

colouring pencils / pens / paints

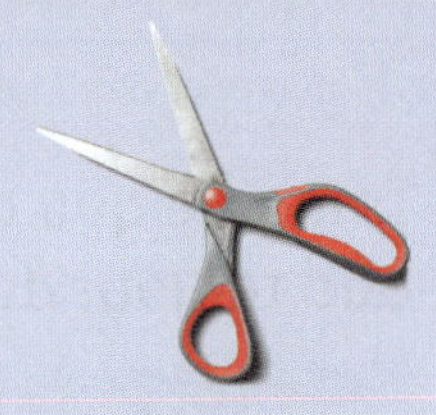

scissors

1 Choose a location to 'hide' your possums.

2 Copy four outlines of the possum onto A4 card.

3 Colour each outline differently. Colour one of them to best blend into your chosen environment.

4 Cut out your possums and place them in the environment. Conduct a test to see how effective your camouflage is. (Journal 1)

TARGETING STEM JOURNAL 5 @ PASCAL PRESS ISBN 978-1-925726-10-7

Possum Outline

1 **a.** Test how long it takes for other students to spot your differently coloured possums.

	Possum 1	Possum 2	Possum 3	Possum 4
Student 1				
Student 2				
Student 3				
Student 4				

b. Which one was hardest to spot? ______________________________

2 Research how other animals are camouflaged. Use some of the ideas to make another camouflaged possum.

3 Read Possum Magic by Mem Fox. Grandma Poss's bush magic changed animals in different ways. What would be the advantages and disadvantages of these adaptations?

	Advantage	Disadvantage
Blue wombat		
Pink kookaburra		
Shrinking emu		
Invisible possum		

DID YOU KNOW?

The US Army is developing an invisibility cloak that guides light around an object rather than reflecting from it. One current problem though is people inside the cloak can't see out!

TARGETING STEM JOURNAL 5 @ PASCAL PRESS ISBN 978-1-925726-10-7

6

Safari park

SCIENCE SSU072, SSU074, SHE061, SIS065, SIS068, SIS071

MATHEMATICS

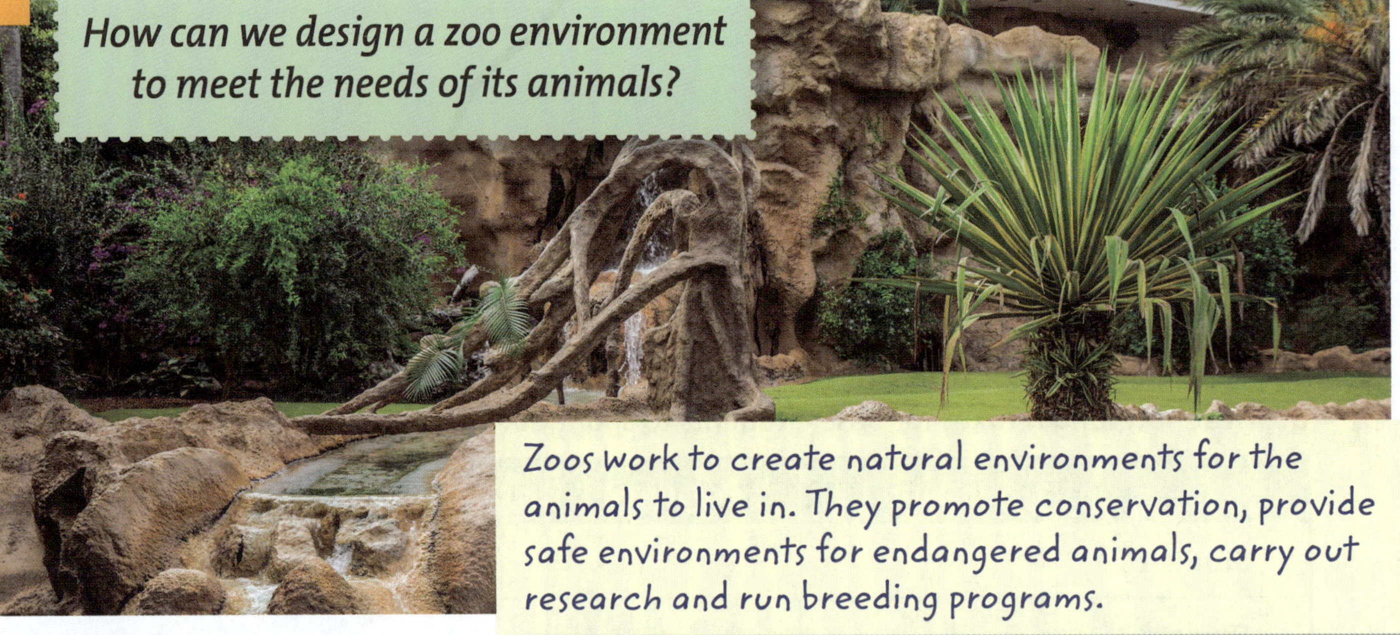

How can we design a zoo environment to meet the needs of its animals?

Zoos work to create natural environments for the animals to live in. They promote conservation, provide safe environments for endangered animals, carry out research and run breeding programs.

What you need

modelling materials

drawing materials

natural materials

1 Complete Journal 1 and 2.

	My animal's environmental needs	Notes
Food sources	Pasture, hay, grains	Grazers
Water sources	Water trough	
Shelter	Shade cover	
Place to raise young	Sheltered nursery paddock	
Other water features	Stream	
Trees / bushes / groundcover	Grass, trees	
Rocks		
Habitat size	Room for at least two	Herd animals

2 Make a small model of your animal. Your environment will need to be to the same scale.

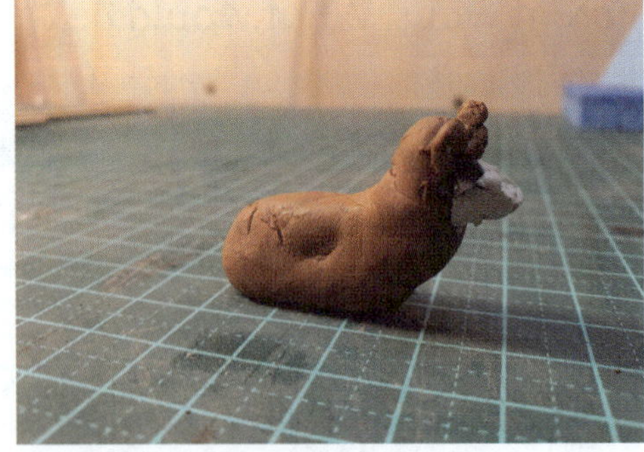

3 Create a detailed plan or model the environment using natural materials.

4 Label the environment to show features such as shelter, food and water sources and places to raise the young.

TARGETING STEM JOURNAL 5 @ PASCAL PRESS ISBN 978-1-925726-10-7

1 Choose an animal to design a natural zoo environment for. Research your animal's environmental needs and record them below.

My animal ______________________ Main biome ________________________

	My animal's environmental needs	Notes
Food sources		
Water sources		
Shelter		
Place to raise young		
Other water features		
Trees / bushes / groundcover		
Rocks		
Habitat size		
Security		

2 Sketch out a design for your animal's environment and label its main features.

DID YOU KNOW?

Tierpark Hagenbeck in Germany was displaying animals in open enclosures rather than cages back in 1907.

What's the matter?

How does filling a balloon with different types of matter affect its properties?

Liquids, solids and gases are different **states of matter** that look, feel and behave in different ways.

What you need

3 balloons | food scales | freezer | water | wet area such as a sink | sand (Journal 3)

1 Fill balloon 1 with water and freeze overnight.

2 Fill balloon 2 with the same amount of water as balloon 1.

3 Blow up balloon 3 to the same size as balloon 2.

4 Make observations of the three balloons. Complete Journal 1.

TARGETING STEM JOURNAL 5 @ PASCAL PRESS ISBN 978-1-925726-10-7

1 Complete the observation chart.

Balloon 1 – solid (ice)	Balloon 2 – liquid (water)	Balloon 3 – gas (air)
Describe the shape of each balloon.		
Describe how each balloon changes when you squeeze it.		
Describe the way each balloon rolls across the desk.		
Describe how the contents behave if the balloon is cut. (Do this in a wet area such as a sink.)		
Describe what happens if you try to put the contents back in.		

2 Use your notes from Journal 1 to complete this chart of properties for solids, liquids and gases.

	Solid	Liquid	Gas	Sand
Has a definite shape				
Spreads out at the bottom of its container				
Spreads out to completely fill its container				
Can be poured				
Changes shape when squeezed				

3 **a.** Fill a balloon with fine sand and repeat the observations from Journal 1.

b. Complete the Sand column in the chart above.

c. Does sand act more like a solid, liquid or gas? Which do you think it is? Explain below.

____

____

4 Stress balls are balloons packed with materials such as flour, fine sand, small beans or rice and tied at the top. Experiment with small amounts of different materials, then make either a **firm stress ball** or a **looser stress ball**. Which one do you prefer?

TARGETING STEM JOURNAL 5 @ PASCAL PRESS ISBN 978-1-925726-10-7

Frozen cold

How cold is frozen cold?

The freezing point is the temperature at which a liquid changes to a solid. The melting point is the temperature at which a solid becomes a liquid.

What you need

two thermometers | cardboard cup with lid | bowl | water | freezer | salt (Journal 5)

1 Complete Journal 1 predictions.

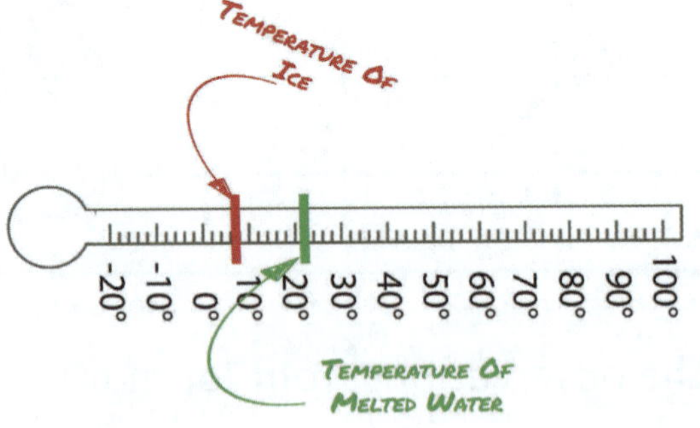

2 Carefully punch a small hole in the side of the cup near the bottom. Seal the hole temporarily with sticky tape or plasticine.

3 Half fill the cup with water. Push thermometer 1 through the straw hole and place in the freezer overnight.

4 Remove the cup from the freezer and place it in the bowl. Record the temperature of the ice on thermometer 1 and the melted water on thermometer 2 in the chart (Journal 2).

TARGETING STEM JOURNAL 5 @ PASCAL PRESS ISBN 978-1-925726-10-7

1 In the experiment you're going to measure the temperature of ice and its melting water. How cold is ice? How cold is melted water? Mark the thermometer below with your predictions.

100° 90° 80° 70° 60° 50° 40° 30° 20° 10° 0° -10° -20°

2 Record the temperature from the two thermometers below.

	0	10 mins	20 mins	30 mins	40 mins	50 mins	60 mins	70 mins	80 mins
Thermometer 1									
Thermometer 2									

3 Plot the temperatures on the graph below. Use a line graph as you are comparing changes over time. Add labels and a title. Use different colours for the two thermometers.

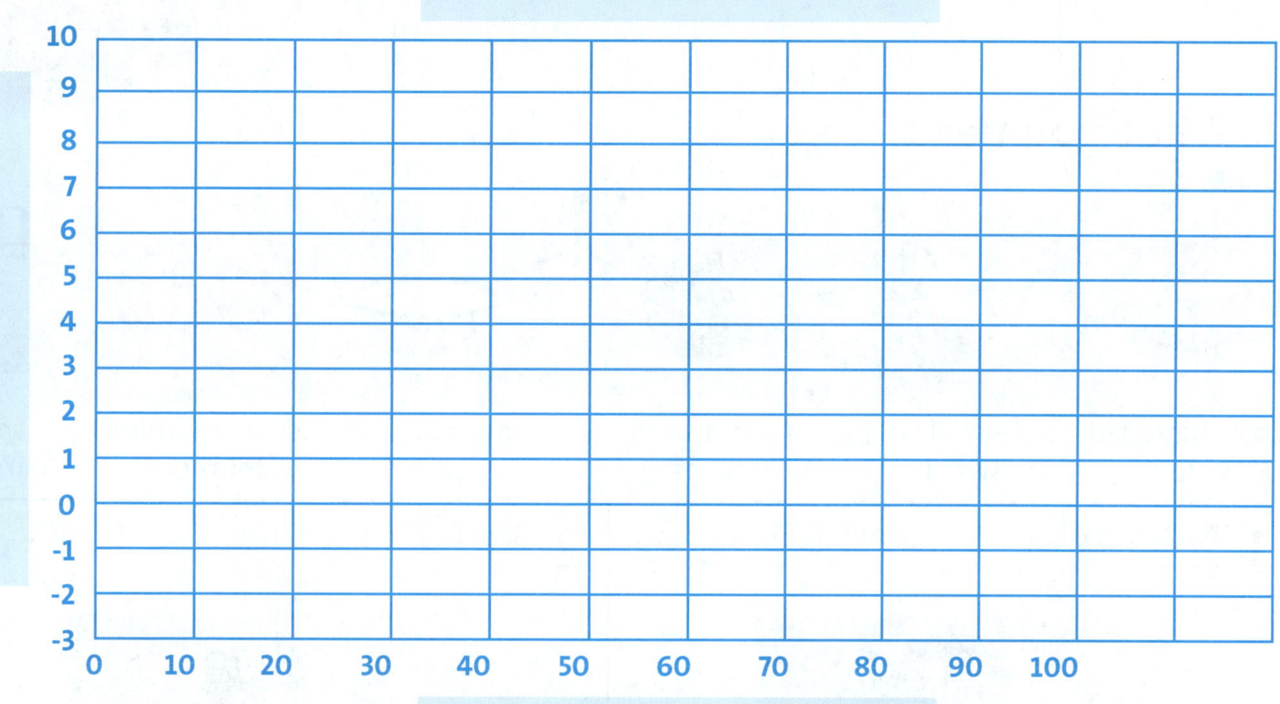

4 What was the temperature of the ice? What was the temperature of the melting water? How accurate were your predictions? Explain below.

5 Why do you think that many countries sprinkle tonnes of salt on icy roads in winter? Test your idea by repeating the experiment but with half a cup of salt added in Step 2 of the directions. Add your results to the graph using a different colour. Describe your observations.

MATTER CHECK Classify ice and water as solid, liquid or gas.

	Solid	Liquid	Gas
Ice			
Water			

TARGETING STEM JOURNAL 5 @ PASCAL PRESS ISBN 978-1-925726-10-7

Better butter

How can we make even better butter?

Shaking thickened cream separates its fat molecules from the liquid. The fat molecules clump together to form butter. The leftover liquid is called buttermilk.

What you need

cold thickened cream | a clean glass jar with lid | measuring cups | strainer | clean marbles (Journal 3) | salt (Journal 4)

1 Pour half a cup of thickened cream into the jar.

2 Seal the lid and shake.

3 While shaking, record your observations in Journal 1.

4 After 15 minutes of shaking, use the strainer to separate the butter from the buttermilk.

TARGETING STEM JOURNAL 5 @ PASCAL PRESS ISBN 978-1-925726-10-7

1 Record the changes you can see, feel and hear as you shake the jar.

Time	See	Feel	Hear

2 Compare the observable properties of the solid butter and the liquid buttermilk.

Property	Butter	Buttermilk
Colour		
Smell		
Taste		
Texture		
Other		

3 Many traditional instructions for making butter include adding 2 or 3 marbles along with the thickened cream. What do you think their purpose is? Write your prediction below, then test it out.

____

4 A little salt is also often added at Step 1 for both taste and preservation. Devise an experiment to check the difference between plain butter (Journal 1) and salted butter (Journal 4).

____

5 Shaking jars can be a very tiring way to make butter, but imagine if you were making a lot of butter! Create a butter-making machine to make the job easier.

Did you know?

Buttermilk is a popular drink in many Indian, Nepalese, Pakistani and Arab households. Buttermilk is also used in making baked goods, ice cream and pancakes.

MATTER CHECK

Classify thickened cream, buttermilk and butter as solid, liquid or gas.

	Solid	Liquid	Gas
Buttermilk			
Butter			
Thickened cream			

TARGETING STEM JOURNAL 5 @ PASCAL PRESS ISBN 978-1-925726-10-7

Gas power

How can we power a boat with gas?

Jet boats are propelled forward by a jet of water being pushed out the back. Jet planes fly by a jet of hot air being pushed out of the engines.

What you need

small plastic bottle with lid

bowl or sink with water

vinegar and baking soda

a skewer or screwdriver

various craft tools and materials (Journal 3)

1 Make a small hole in the base of the plastic bottle near the edge.

2 Lay the bottle on its side, small hole up.

3 Add half a cup of vinegar and tilt it to the bottom. Add a heaped tablespoon of baking soda.

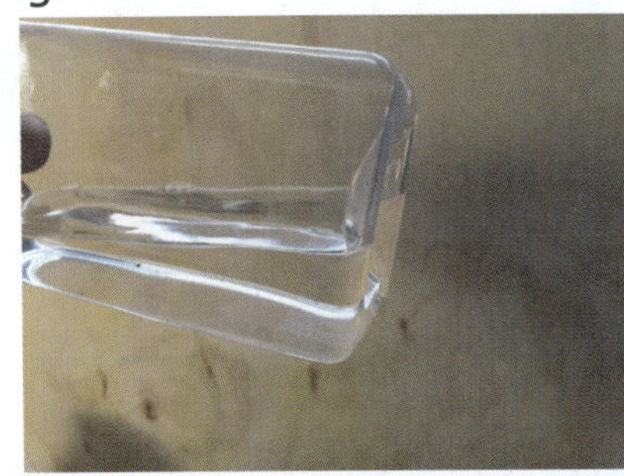

4 Replace and tighten the lid, then push the bottle into the water, small hole first.

TARGETING STEM JOURNAL 5 @ PASCAL PRESS ISBN 978-1-925726-10-7

1 Complete Steps 1–4. Observe and record below what happened when you pushed the bottle under the water.

---

2 When baking soda and vinegar are mixed, the reaction creates carbon dioxide, a colourless and usually odourless gas. What evidence was there of a gas coming out from the hole?

---

3 Design a boat powered by carbon dioxide in the space below. Use the plastic bottle from the experiment as your starting point. Ideas:

- Add an exhaust pipe (or two) to concentrate the gas flow.
- Add a keel to keep the boat from turning sideways.
- Change the shape of the lid to make it more streamlined.
- Invent a better way to mix the vinegar and baking soda.

MATTER CHECK

Classify vinegar, baking soda and carbon dioxide as solid, liquid or gas.

	Solid	Liquid	Gas
Vinegar			
Baking soda			
Carbon dioxide			

DID YOU KNOW?

- Carbon dioxide is a greenhouse gas. The amount of carbon dioxide in the atmosphere has been increasing and it is contributing to climate change.
- Dry ice, used to create fog effects in movies, is solid carbon dioxide.
- Carbon dioxide is the 'fizzy' in soft drinks.

Take the pressure down

How can we measure changes in air pressure?

Air pressure is the force exerted by the weight of air over a surface area. The barometer in the picture measures changes in the air pressing on the cylinder behind the hands.

What you need

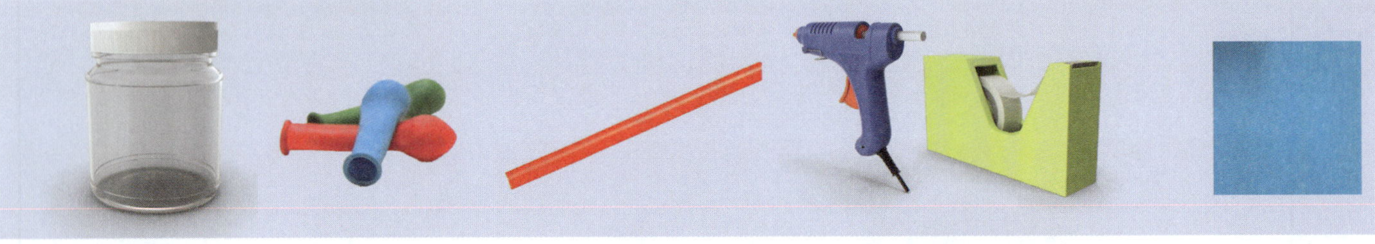

glass jar, balloon, straw, hot glue gun / sticky tape, card

1 Cut the base off the balloon and stretch it across the mouth of the jar.

2 Attach the straw to one side of the balloon. If using the hot-glue gun, put the glue on the straw, then press it onto the balloon.

3 Point the straw towards the card and mark its current position.

4 Set the barometer in a place that stays the same temperature most of the time.

TARGETING STEM JOURNAL 5 @ PASCAL PRESS ISBN 978-1-925726-10-7

1 Test the barometer.

a. Press down on top of the balloon on the edge away from the straw. What happens?

____

b. Pull up the centre of the balloon. What happens?

____

2 Observe the barometer over a week. Record your observations below. In the bottom row record the weather for that time of the day: hot, warm, cold, cloudy, rainy, stormy.

Day	1		2		3		4		5	
	Morning	Afternoon	Morning	Afternoon	Morning	Afternoon	Morning	Afternoon	Morning	Afternoon
Higher										
Same										
Lower										

3 a. What do you think is happening on those days when the straw is pointing higher?

____

b. What do you think is happening on those days when the straw is pointing lower?

____

c. Can you see any connection between changes in the barometer and changes in the weather?

____

4 Look at the picture of a barometer.

a. Label the 'straw'.

b. Label the 'jar'.

c. Label the 'card'.

d. Is it showing high or low pressure?

____

TDEK011, TDEK012, TDEK013

TECH & DESIGN

DIGITAL TECH

TARGETING STEM JOURNAL 5 @ PASCAL PRESS ISBN 978-1-925726-10-7

Liquid speed bumps

How can we make a speed bump that hardens when you drive too fast?

Speed bumps are used to slow or 'calm' traffic. They can be dangerous though for motorcycles and vehicles that are low to the ground even at low speed.

What you need

1 cup cornflour | ½ cup of water | mixing bowl | spoon | zip-lock bags (Journal 4) | large toy car (Journal 4)

1 Complete Journal 1 by testing the two ingredients.

2 Pour the cornflour into the mixing bowl and add half the water.

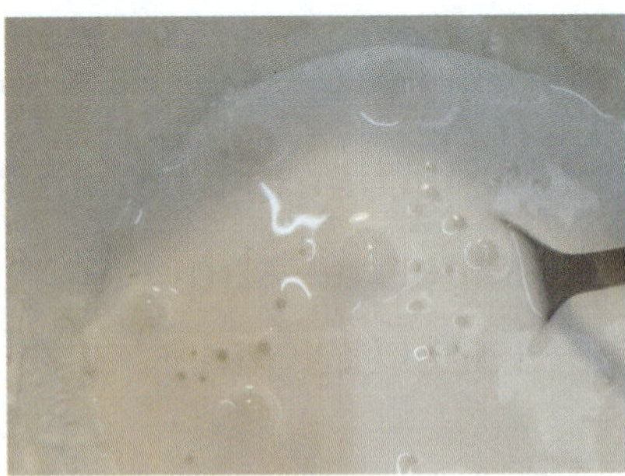

3 Use your hands to mix it thoroughly as you add the rest of the water.

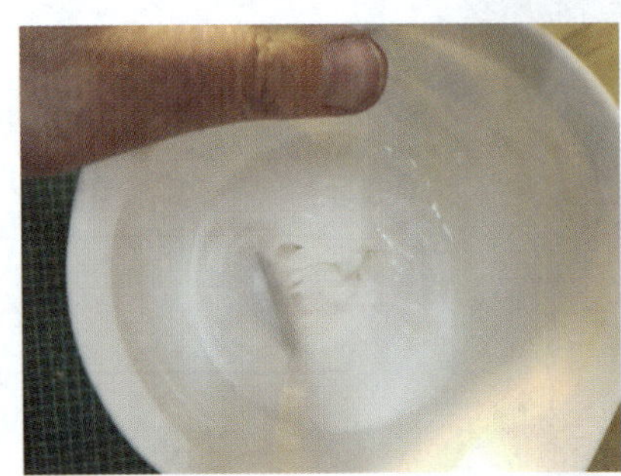

4 Complete Journal 2 and test the mixture.

TARGETING STEM JOURNAL 5 @ PASCAL PRESS ISBN 978-1-925726-10-7

1 Before you mix the cornflour and water gently push, pat and stir them. Write your observations below.

Property	Cornflour	Water
Can be heaped up		
Can be poured		
Can be held in the hand		

2 Test the mixture. What happens if you:

a. Push your hand in gently?

____

b. Stir the mixture gently?

____

c. Pat hard with your hand?

____

d. Stir the mixture vigorously?

____

e. Grab a handful of mixture?

____

3 Not all liquids take the shape of the container they are poured into. Some liquids will even act like solids when they are hit while some get runnier if you shake them. These liquids are called non-Newtonian fluids. (See Did you know?) Visit en.wikipedia.org/wiki/Non-Newtonian_fluid and scroll down to the examples. Below, list other non-Newtonian fluids.

____

____

4 Read the question above the main picture and the speed bump information below. How could you make a speed bump that is soft at low speeds but harder at fast speeds? Sketch out a design that uses the cornflour mixture and the zip-lock bags or use your own idea. Make and test your design with the toy car.

DID YOU KNOW?

Sir Isaac Newton was a famous scientist who lived nearly 300 years ago. He researched liquids and their properties and described how they flowed depending on temperature and pressure. Those liquids that don't follow his 'rules' are called non-Newtonian fluids.

13

SCIENCE SSU074, SSU076, SHE061, SIS065, SIS068, SIS071

MATHEMATICS MMG084, MSP095, MSP096

A year's a long time

What you need

school oval | tape measure | stopwatch | marker cones | partner | calculator (Journal 4)

1 Use a cone to mark the middle of the oval. This is the 'sun'.

2 Place 8 cones in a 1m radius circle around the sun. This represents Earth's orbit. (See Astronomical Units.)

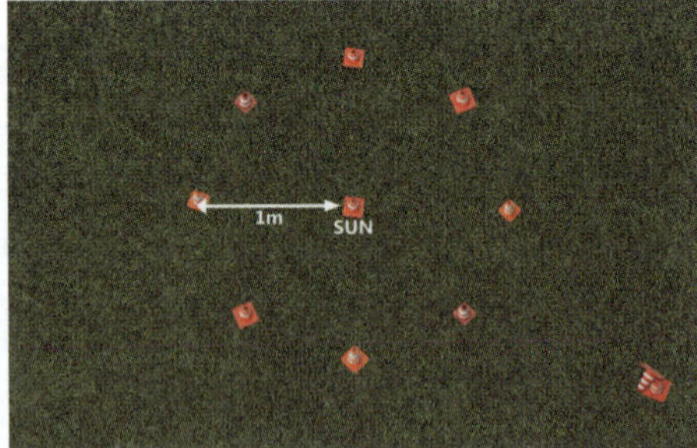

3 Choose a starting cone. Time your partner running around the circle, touching each cone in turn. Record your results in Journal 1.

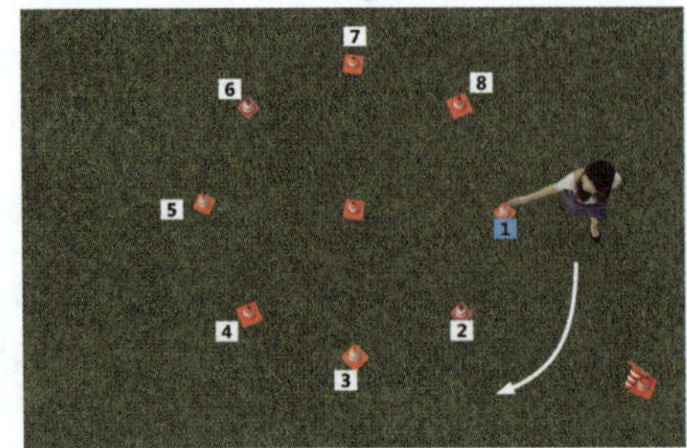

4 Set out the cones in a 5.2m radius circle and complete Journal 2.

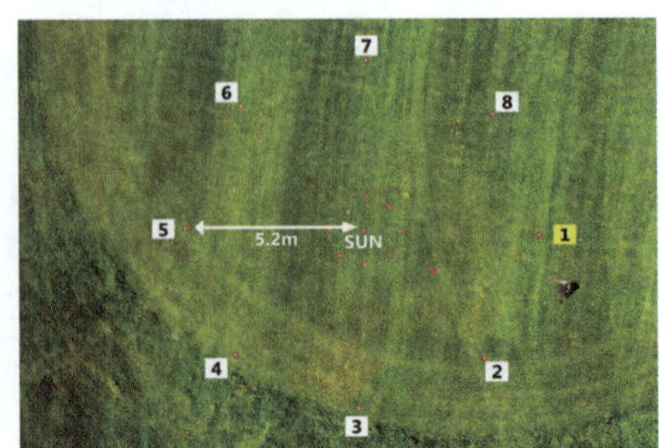

TARGETING STEM JOURNAL 5 @ PASCAL PRESS ISBN 978-1-925726-10-7

1 Complete the table below with the times taken to complete one lap of the 'sun'.

Planet	Distance of cones from 'sun' in scale AU	Time in seconds for running one lap
Earth	1m	

2 Jupiter is a lot further out from the sun and travels at half the speed of Earth. To model this, move the cones out to 5.2m and time your partner walking rather than running. Record the result below.

Planet	Distance of cones from 'sun' in scale AU	Time in seconds for walking one lap
Jupiter	5.2m	

3 Use a calculator to work out how much longer the Jupiter lap took by dividing the Journal 2 answer (Jupiter) by the Journal 1 answer (Earth).

2 Jupiter's walking lap (secs)

1 Earth's running lap (secs)

= ____________ times longer

4 **a.** From your calculations, how many times longer is the 'Jupiter year'?

____

b. Check the answer section at the back of the book. How much longer is it?

____

c. Suggest why your answer is different. Think about your measurements, timing, walking and running.

____

ASTRONOMICAL UNITS

Distances in the solar system are very, very large! Rather than using kilometres, astronomers sometimes use Astronomical Units or AU. One AU is the distance from the Sun to the Earth – about 150 million km. In our model, 1m represents 1AU.

SCALE MODEL

This activity uses a very rough (inaccurate!) scale model of the solar system. The cones are a rough model of a planet's orbital path. The student running or walking is a rough representation of the planet's speed.

Happy birthdays to me!

How many birthdays would you have had if you were born on a different planet??

Your birthday is the anniversary of your birth date and is celebrated after Earth has orbited the sun once. Other planets take different amounts of time to orbit the sun and your number of birthdays would be different on other planets.

1 Open a new worksheet. Complete Journal 1 a.

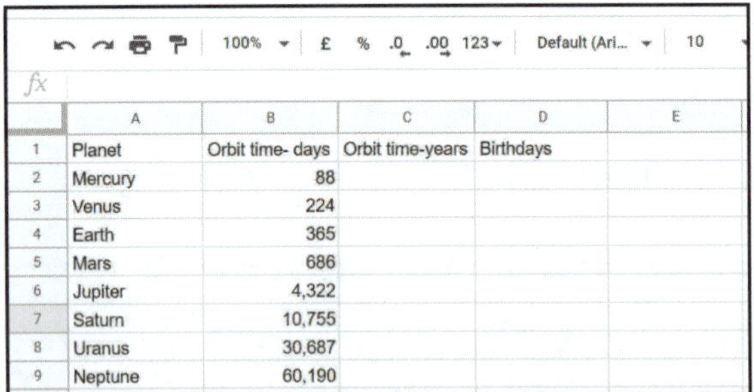

	A	B	C	D	E
1	Planet	Orbit time- days	Orbit time-years	Birthdays	
2	Mercury	88			
3	Venus	224			
4	Earth	365			
5	Mars	686			
6	Jupiter	4,322			
7	Saturn	10,755			
8	Uranus	30,687			
9	Neptune	60,190			

2 Select C2. Type the formula =B2/365.

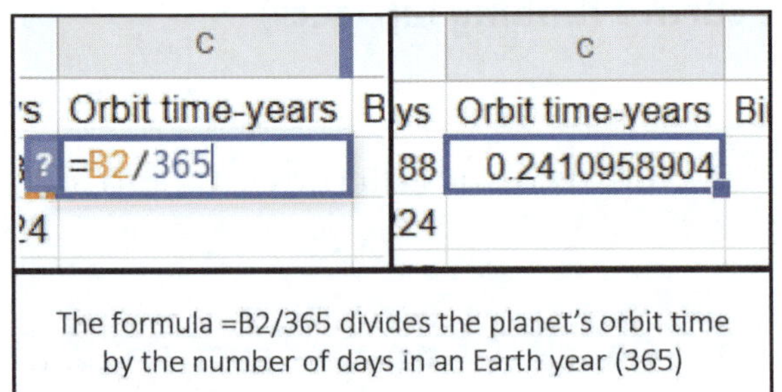

The formula =B2/365 divides the planet's orbit time by the number of days in an Earth year (365)

3 Select C2. Click the blue square in the corner of the cell and drag down to B9.

Orbit time-years
0.2410958904
0.6136986301
1
1.879452055
11.84109589
29.46575342

4 Select D2. Type the formula =10/C2.

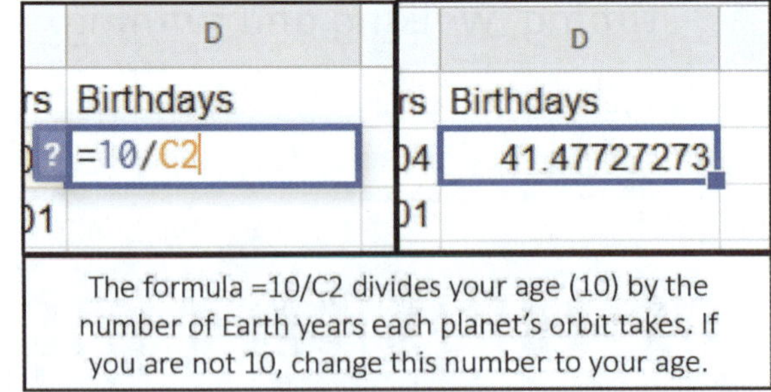

The formula =10/C2 divides your age (10) by the number of Earth years each planet's orbit takes. If you are not 10, change this number to your age.

5 Select D2. Click the blue square in the corner of the cell and drag down to B9.

Birthdays
41.47727273
16.29464286
10
5.320699708
0.8445164276
0.3393770339

6 Select B2-C9. Decrease the number of decimal places to 2. Save your spreadsheet as Planet Birthdays.

Decrease decimal places

=B2/365

	A	B	C	D
1	Planet	Orbit time- days	Orbit time-years	Birthdays
2	Mercury	88	0.24	41.48
3	Venus	224	0.61	16.29
4	Earth	365	1.00	10.00
5	Mars	686	1.88	5.32

SCIENCE SSU074

MATHEMATICS MMG084, MMG087

1 The table below shows the time (in days) that it takes each planet to orbit the Sun.

a. Copy the headings and data to a new spreadsheet.

Planet	Orbit time- days	Orbit time-years	Birthdays
Mercury	88		
Venus	224		
Earth	365		
Mars	686		
Jupiter	4,322		
Saturn	10,755		
Uranus	30,687		
Neptune	60,190		

b. Copy the data from the spreadsheet into the table above.

2 Use your table to answer the questions. On which planet do you have:

a. The correct number of birthdays? ______________________

b. The most birthdays? ______________________

c. The least birthdays? ______________________

d. About half the number of birthdays? ______________________

e. About one birthday? ______________________

3 The average Australian life span is around 82 years.

a. Change the formula in D1 to = 82/C2. Shift-select C2-C9 and fill down the column.

b. How many birthdays would an 82-year-old have on Mercury?

c. On which planet would an 82-year-old be closest to their first birthday?

4 If we had birthdays less often, they would probably become much more important. Design a birthday cake or card for someone about to have their first birthday on Saturn. Include the person's age on the other planets.

Mapping the solar system

How could we create a scaled down model of the solar system in Australia?

The distances between the planets in our solar system are huge so even a small model will take up a lot of space.

What you need

https://www.google.com/earth/

1 Start Google Earth and navigate to Australia. Enlarge the map so WA fills most of the screen.

2 Click the Projects icon and click New Project. Click Create KML file. Edit the title and change to 'Mapping the Solar System'.

3 Click New Feature > Add placemark. Click the map near Carnavron.

4 Change the Place title to 'The Sun'. Click Save.

TARGETING STEM JOURNAL 5 @ PASCAL PRESS ISBN 978-1-925726-10-7

1 Complete the table with the scaled down distance from the sun.

Planet	Distance from the Sun	Scaled distance: 1 million km = 1km
Mercury	52.2 million km	52.2km
Venus	108.1 million km	108.1km
Earth	147.2 million km	
Mars	217.8 million km	
Jupiter	770.7 million km	
Saturn	1,427 million km	1,427km
Uranus	2,572 million km	
Neptune	4,529 million km	

2 Add Saturn to the map.

a. Click the 'Measure distance and area' icon.

b. Click 'The Sun' and move the crosshairs until the distance is close to 1,427km. Press Enter.

c. Remember the spot! Click 'New feature' again and 'Add placemark'. Click where the end of the line in step 7 was. Change the title to 'Saturn'.

3 Repeat for the other planets.

- Zoom in for the four planets closest to the Sun. It will make it easier to measure the smaller distances.
- Try to keep your planets in a straight line!
- You may have a problem with Neptune!

4 Add pictures to your planets.

a. Click 'Saturn' in the Project panel and click the Edit icon.

b. Click the Add photo icon then search for Saturn by clicking the Google Image Search button.

c. Choose your photo and click 'Select'.

d. Click 'Saturn' on your map to see the picture.

5 Some countries have 'Solar System' roads with markers along the way to show where the planets would be on a smaller scale. In fact, Coonabarabran in NSW has the world's largest! (solarsystemdrive.com) Use Google Earth to create your own 'Solar System Drive' using your school as the sun and measuring distances along the road system.

DID YOU KNOW?

On this scale, Earth, which is 12,742km in diameter would be 12.7m in diameter.

Finding Venus

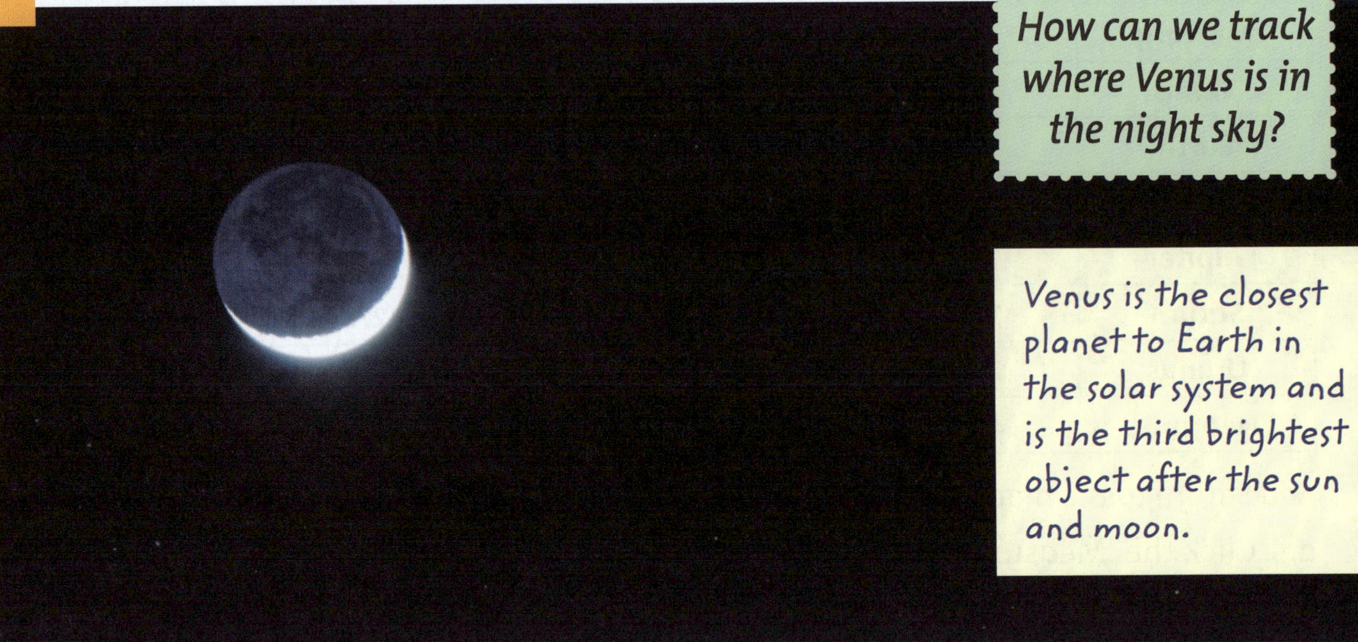

How can we track where Venus is in the night sky?

Venus is the closest planet to Earth in the solar system and is the third brightest object after the sun and moon.

What you need

the night sky

local area map or compass (Journal 1)

1 Navigate to the website stellarium-web.org.

2 Click 'Planets Tonight' and check if Venus is visible.

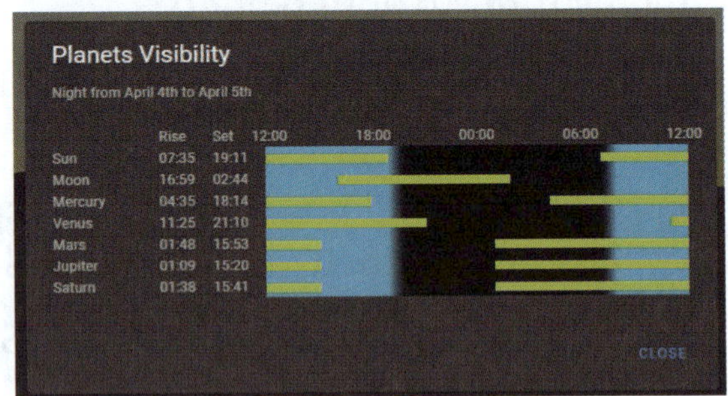

3 Type 'Venus' in the Search field and press Enter. Click 'Planet'.

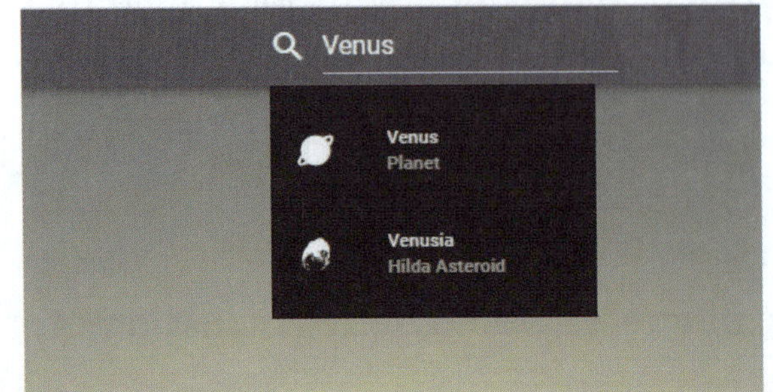

4 Click the clock and change the time to when it is dark. Make a note of where Venus will be.

TARGETING STEM JOURNAL 5 @ PASCAL PRESS ISBN 978-1-925726-10-7

1 a. Use the local area map or compass to locate North, South, East and West. Use the information from the table to locate and view Venus.

b. Write in the date and time in the table. Draw a sketch showing the horizon, any buildings or trees and the position of Venus.

Date	Time	Date	Time
Venus		Venus	
Date	Time	Date	Time
Venus		Venus	
Date	Time	Date	Time
Venus		Venus	

2 Complete observations for five more nights and fill in the table.

3 Explain what you notice about Venus's position and time in the sky.

____

____

NOTES

Stellarium asks for your location so it can show you the correct view. If you block this, you will need to add your location in manually.

DID YOU KNOW?

- Venus orbits the sun in the opposite direction to all the other planets.
- Venus spins so slowly its day is longer than its year!

TARGETING STEM JOURNAL 5 @ PASCAL PRESS ISBN 978-1-925726-10-7

Solar system stop-motion

How could we make a video to show the orbits of Earth and Mars around the sun?

Earth and Mars, along with Mercury and Venus, are called terrestrial planets because they are made up of rocks or metals.

What you need

project card (A2 size)

split pin

tablet with stop motion app

tools: scissors, marker pens, ruler, protractor and drawing compass

modelling clay

1 Locate the centre of your card. Use the compass to draw a 15cm radius circle and a 22cm radius circle.

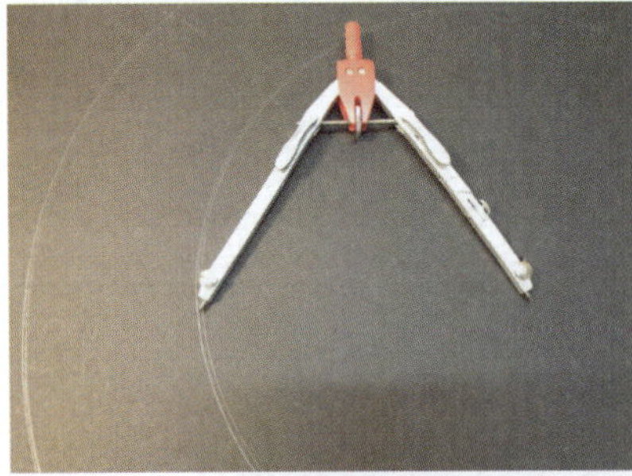

2 Label the smaller circle 'Earth' and the larger one 'Mars'.

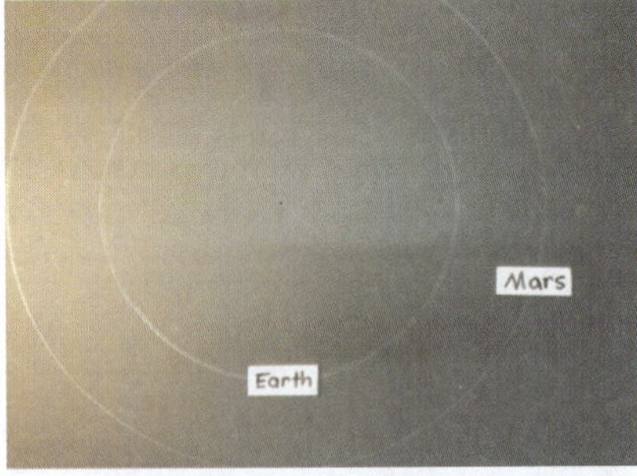

3 Rule a line across the circles through the centre. Use the protractor to mark every 30 degrees around the large circle. Label the marks 1–12 (like a clock).

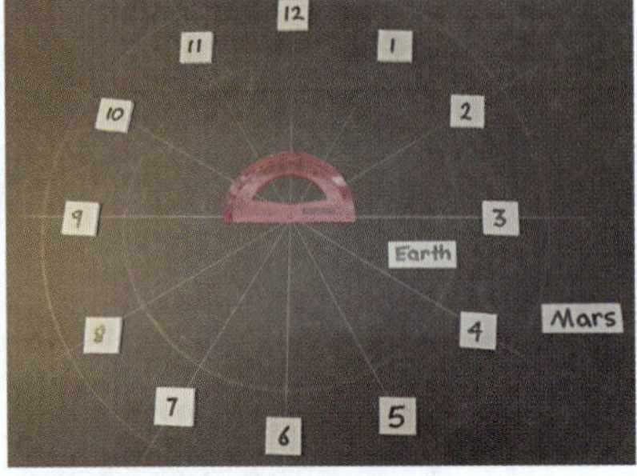

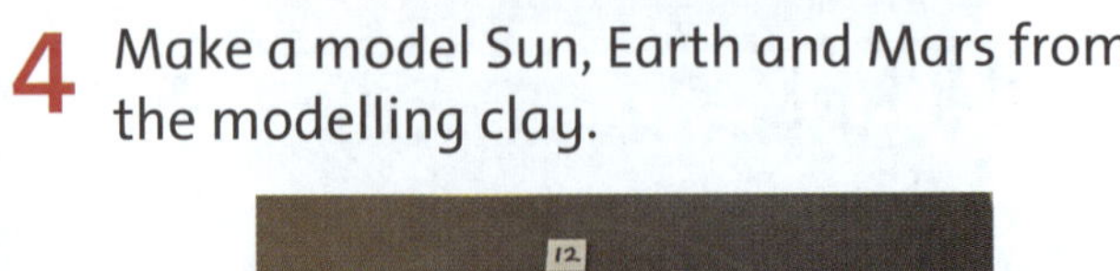

4 Make a model Sun, Earth and Mars from the modelling clay.

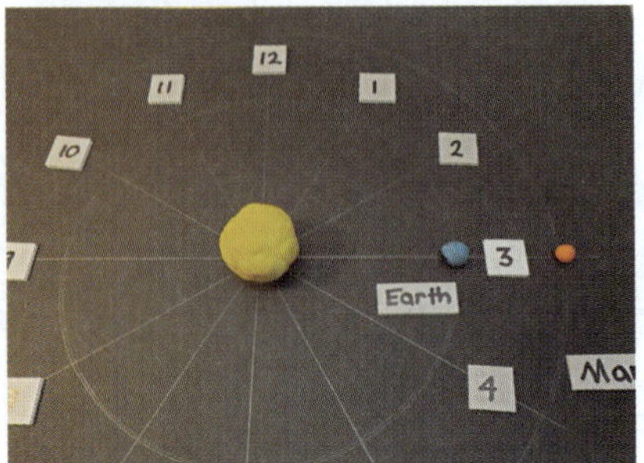

TARGETING STEM JOURNAL 5 @ PASCAL PRESS ISBN 978-1-925726-10-7

1 From Unit 14 *(Happy birthdays to me!)* we know that Earth (365 days) orbits the sun about twice as quickly as Mars (686 days). Both planets orbit counter-clockwise.

a. Place the model Sun in the centre of your card. Place the Earth and Mars models on their orbits at '12 o'clock'.

b. Move Earth to 11. Move Mars half-way to 11½.

c. Move Earth to 10. Move Mars to 11.

d. Move Earth to 9. Move Mars to 10½.

e. Continue moving Earth and Mars. Complete the table below.

Earth	12	11	10	9	8	7	6	5	4	3	2	1	12
Mars	12	11½	11	10½	10								6

f. Describe the pattern of where Mars is compared to Earth.

____

g. Continue the moves until Mars returns home to 12.

Earth	12	11	10	9	8	7	6	5	4	3	2	1	12
Mars	6	5½	5							1½	1	12½	12

2 Set up your tablet so it can record the whole model. Repeat Journal 1, but this time take a photo each time you move the two planets.

a. At what position are Mars and Earth the closest? ____________________

b. At what position are Mars and Earth the furthest apart? ______________

3 Add Venus to your model.

a. Draw Venus's orbit with a 10cm radius.

b. Venus orbits 1½ times more quickly than the Earth. Every time you move the Earth one marker, your Venus model has to move clockwise 1½. As mentioned in Unit 16, it orbits clockwise – the opposite direction to Earth. Practise moving the three planets and fill in the chart.

Earth	12	11	10	9	8	7	6	5	4	3	2	1	12
Venus	12	1½	3	4½	6				12	1½			

4 Create a stop motion animation of the three planets' movements. Do they ever all line up together?

SCALE MODELS

The circles represent the orbits of the planets. They have been scaled down so that 10 million km is represented by 1cm.

Super solar marshmallow-melter

How can we melt marshmallows using the sun?

Solar cookers convert the sun's direct and reflected rays into heat energy that cooks the food. They are one way of capturing the sun's energy.

What you need

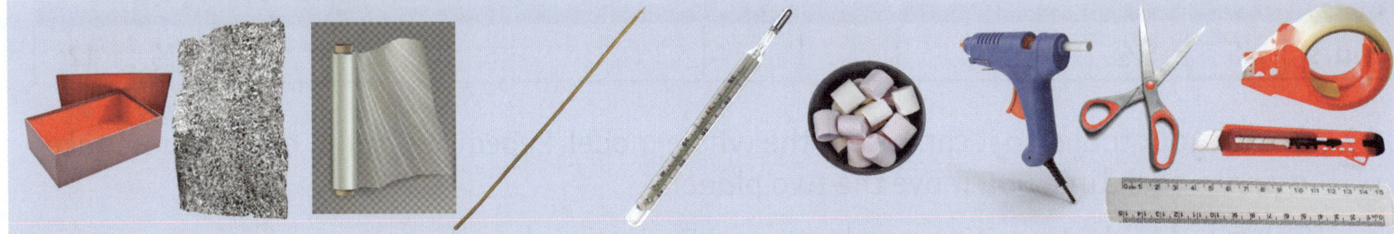

shoebox with a lid | aluminium foil | plastic wrap | wooden skewer | thermometers (Journal 1) | marshmallows | tools: hot glue gun, sticky tape, craft knife, scissors, ruler

1 Cut out a rectangular hole in the lid.

2 Cover the hole with plastic wrap.

3 Line the inside with aluminium foil.

4 Push a skewer through from one side to the other.

TARGETING STEM JOURNAL 5 @ PASCAL PRESS ISBN 978-1-925726-10-7

1 Test your solar cooker. Place the cooker with a thermometer inside out in the sun. Place a second thermometer in the shade of the box. Record the temperature readings over two hours.

Minutes	10	20	30	40	50	60	70	80	90	100	110	120
Thermometer 1												
Thermometer 2												

2 **a.** Plot the two sets of temperatures in different colours on the graph below. Add a heading and labels.

b. Explain the differences between the two thermometers.

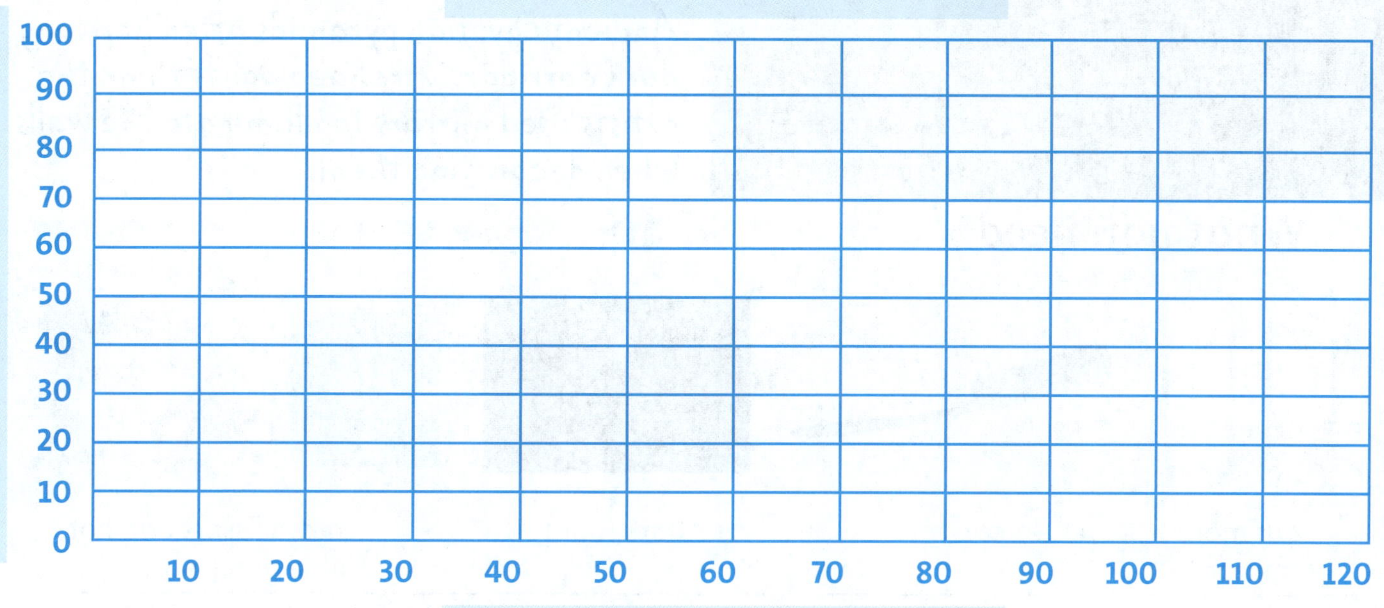

3 Slide a marshmallow onto the skewer and place in the sun. Describe what happens.

____

4 Look at the main photograph. What is the shiny screen for? Why is the inside of the cooker a dark colour? Add these features and your own ideas to improve your cooker and make it work more efficiently.

DID YOU KNOW?

More energy from the sun strikes Earth each hour than the whole world uses in total in a year.

In 2018, 5% of Australia's electricity was solar generated.

TECH & DESIGN TDEK011, TDEK012

DIGITAL TECH TDIK008

Pyramid painting

How can we use mirrors to light up the inside of a pyramid?

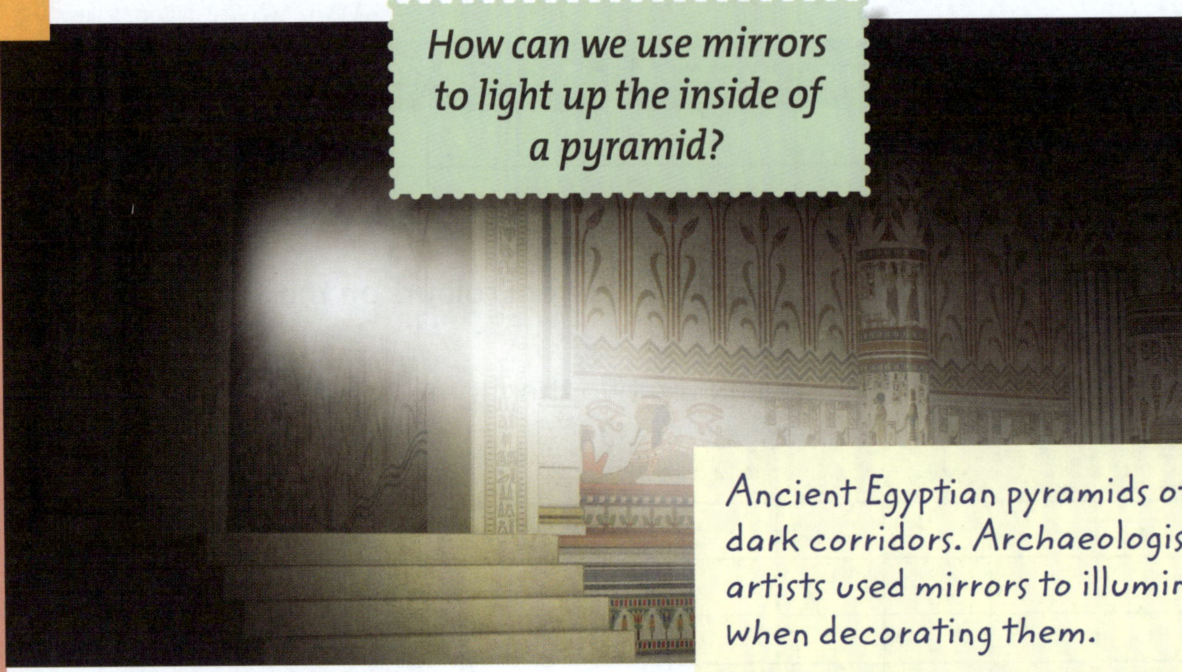

Ancient Egyptian pyramids often had long, dark corridors. Archaeologists think the artists used mirrors to illuminate the walls when decorating them.

What you need

2 or more mirrors | torch | dark room | card, scissors and hot glue gun (Journal 3)

1 Place the 'sun' (torch) securely on a flat surface such as a desk.

2 Choose a location in the 'pyramid' (the room) to illuminate.

3 Place a mirror in the path of the 'sun' and reflect the light to the chosen location.

4 Try a different location that needs two mirrors to reach.

TARGETING STEM JOURNAL 5 @ PASCAL PRESS ISBN 978-1-925726-10-7

1 Draw a plan of the room showing the position of the 'sun', the two mirrors and the location.

2 Work out where you would place mirrors to reflect the sun onto the artwork in the pyramid plans below.

3 Construct a model of pyramid tunnels.

a. Glue strips of card onto a thick base to create the walls.
b. Attach small mirrors to reflect the beam around the corridors.
c. Glue some Egyptian artwork at the end of the tunnel.
d. Illuminate your artwork using the sun.

DID YOU KNOW?

The Pyramids at Giza were once covered by polished limestone, making the whole monument a giant mirror! Archaeologists think mirrors were used as there is no evidence of smoke from torches on the decorations.

Waterdrop microscope

How can we use a drop of water as a microscope?

A microscope is an instrument that uses lenses to make small objects look larger by magnifying them.

What you need

card | aluminium foil | pin | petroleum jelly (for example, Vaseline) | torch (Journal 2) | tools: hole punch, scissors, glue

1 Punch a hole in the centre of the card. (4–5mm in diameter)

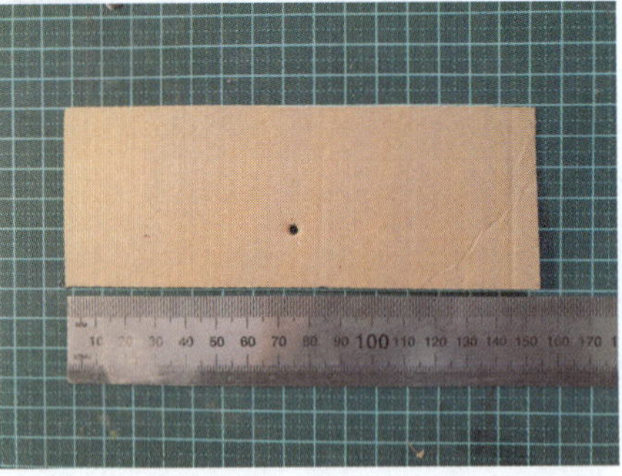

2 Glue the foil around the hole.

3 Use the pin to make a small hole in the foil.

4 Carefully smooth petroleum jelly around (but not in) the hole on both sides.

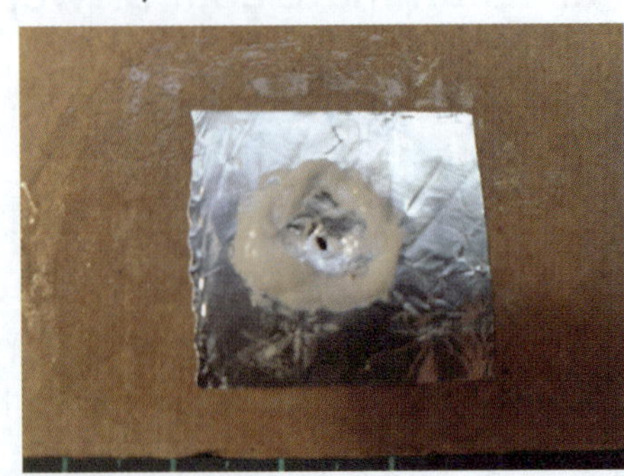

TARGETING STEM JOURNAL 5 @ PASCAL PRESS ISBN 978-1-925726-10-7

1 **a.** Hold the card over a leaf. Describe what you can see through the hole.

____

b. Carefully place a single drop of water onto the hole. It should fit inside with the petroleum jelly keeping it from spreading. Describe what you can see through the waterdrop-covered hole now.

____

2 Try placing the object on an upturned torch to make it easier to see.

a. Rest the torch on its end.

b. Rest the object (transparent or translucent) on the torch's front cover.

c. Hold the waterdrop microscope over the torch.

3 Examine a variety of objects with your microscope and make sketches of what you see below. Some ideas to examine: pepper, soil, feathers, pencil tip, pond water, hair

DID YOU KNOW?

Antonie Philips van Leeuwenhoek was a Dutch scientist born in 1623. He made his own microscopes and was the first person to observe and write about bacteria and blood cells.

TARGETING STEM JOURNAL 5 @ PASCAL PRESS ISBN 978-1-925726-10-7

21

Camera obscura

How can we make a cardboard tube projector?

The 'camera obscura', also called a pinhole camera, projects the image of an outside scene onto a screen in a darkened space.

SCIENCE SSU074, SSU076, SHE061, SIS065, SIS068, SIS071

MATHEMATICS MMG084, MMG090, MSP095, MSP096

What you need

cardboard tube, aluminium foil, tracing paper, magnifying glass (Journal 4), tools: scissors, craft knife, ruler, glue, sticky tape

1 Measure and then cut off the first 5cm of the tube.

2 Cover the end of the shorter piece with aluminium foil and stick it down.

3 Cover the end of the longer piece with tracing paper and stick it down.

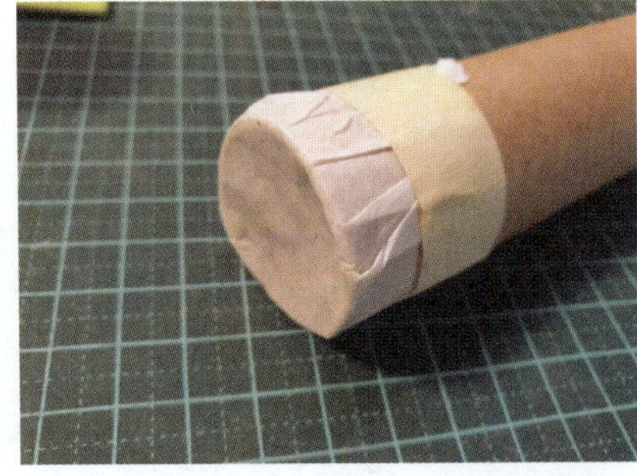

4 Stick the two pieces back together again with sticky tape.

TARGETING STEM JOURNAL 5 @ PASCAL PRESS ISBN 978-1-925726-10-7

1 a Look through the uncovered end at a bright scene. What can you see?

____

b Use a pin to make a tiny hole in the centre of the foil. Look at a bright scene. What do you see on the screen?

____

2 Label the diagram below with the words: light ray from head, light ray from feet, pinhole, screen, upside down image

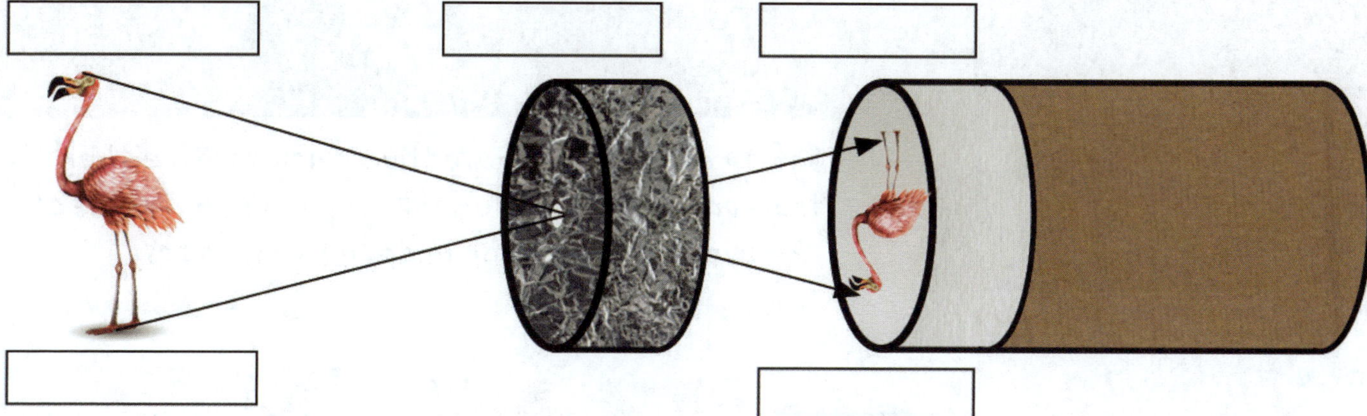

3 The main picture shows tourists viewing a camera obscura in Havana, the capital of Cuba.

- a What scene do you think they are looking at?
- b Where do you think the 'pinhole' is that creates the image?
- c How do you think they turned the image from vertical to horizontal? (Think Egyptian pyramid decorators!)

3 Try this in your classroom with the lights turned off.

- a Hold the magnifying glass up to the window.
- b Hold a piece of paper behind it.
- c Move the paper away from the magnifying glass until you see an image.
- d Describe the image you see on the paper. How does it compare to the one on the screen in your camera obscura?

DID YOU KNOW?

The term 'camera obscura' comes from the old Latin words for *chamber* (camera) and *dark* (obscura).

The only flamingo species found in North America is in Cuba.

DIY safety goggles

How can we make a pair of safety goggles that can be used in both very dark and very bright laboratories?

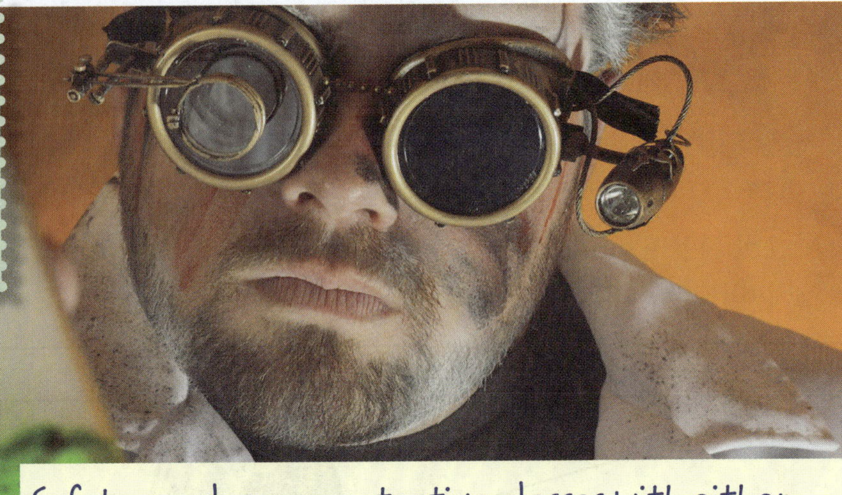

Safety goggles are protective glasses with either transparent or translucent eyepieces that protect the eyes when working in dangerous places.

What you need

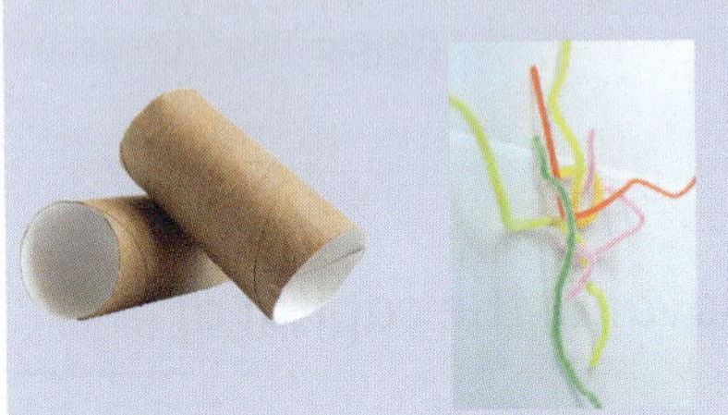

cardboard tube

pipe cleaners or coated gardening wire

card

clear plastic wrap

cellophane

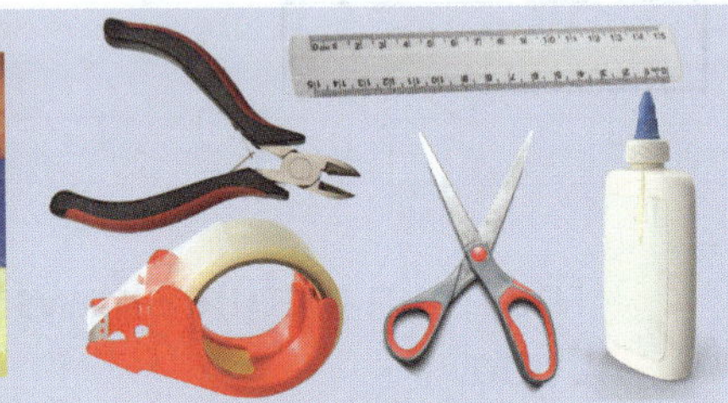

tools: scissors, glue, sticky tape, wire-cutters, ruler

1 Cut two 5cm sections of tube for the eyepieces.

2 Complete Journal 1. Cut out the front of the goggles using your measurements.

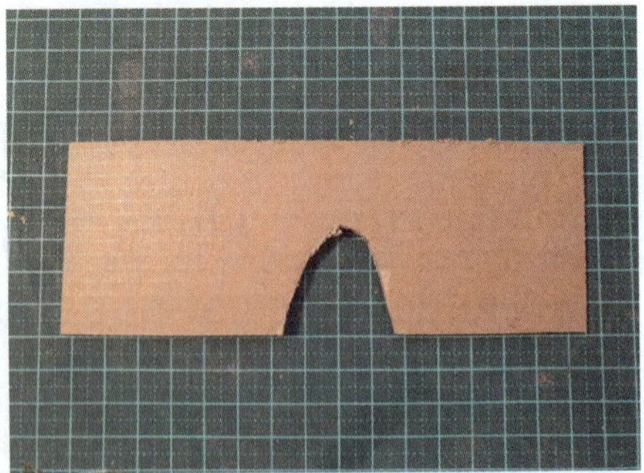

3 Trace around the eyepieces on the goggle fronts. Cut out holes so they fit.

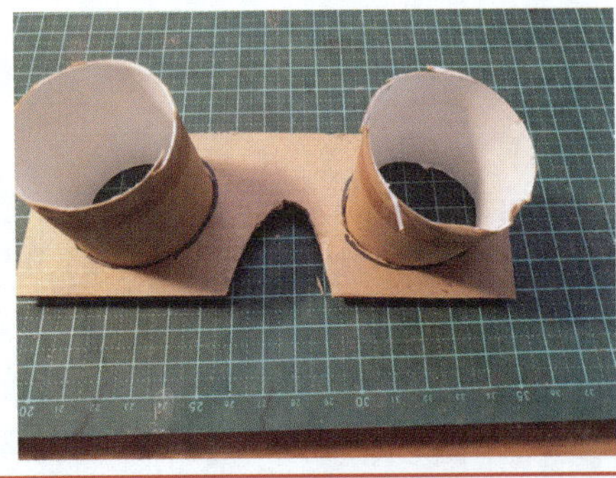

4 Attach wire frames to fit around your ears.

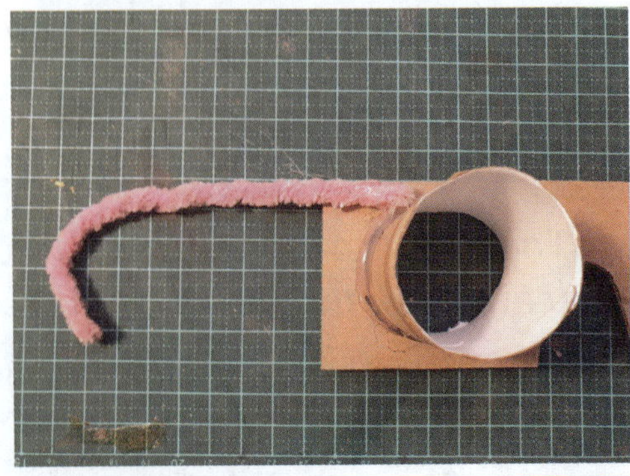

 ISBN 978-1-925726-10-7

1 With the help of a partner, measure your head.

   a Width from the right side of face to the left ______________________
   b Height from the top of eyebrows to the tip of nose ________________
   c Distance from the right side of your face to the right eye ____________
   d Distance from the left side of your face to the left eye ______________
   e Distance from the top of eyebrows to the bridge of nose ____________

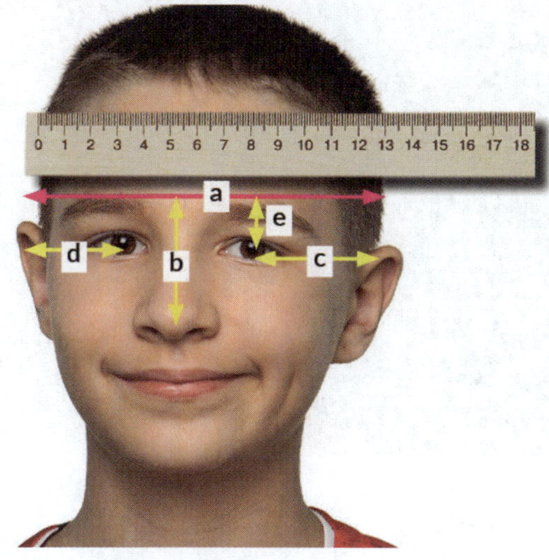

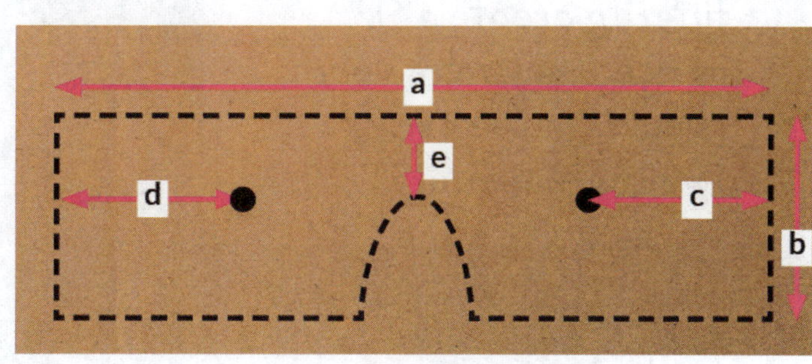

2 a Experiment with layers of plastic wrap and cellophane to create the best eyepiece filters for each laboratory. Write your results below.

Brightly-lit laboratory	Dimly-lit laboratory

   b Finish your goggles by adding the filters to the eye pieces.

3 Redesign the goggles so that an opaque shield can be dropped down over both lenses to leave Professor Pernicious completely in the dark.

Professor Pernicious's design criteria

1. The goggles must be cheap and fashionable.
2. I need to use them in both dimly lit and very bright laboratories.
3. I don't want to bother swapping out filters, just let me shut one eye and open the other.

DEFINITIONS

transparent: allows all light to pass through

translucent: allows some light to pass through

opaque: allows no light to pass through

Do not look directly at the sun with or without sunglasses. Your eye's lens can be damaged from both the sun's visible light and UV light.

23

Anaglyph 3D glasses

How can we make and view 3D pictures?

Anaglyph 3D glasses use one red and one blue filter to create a 3D image. They were very popular in the early twentieth century.

SCIENCE SSU076, SHE061, SIS065

What you need

card

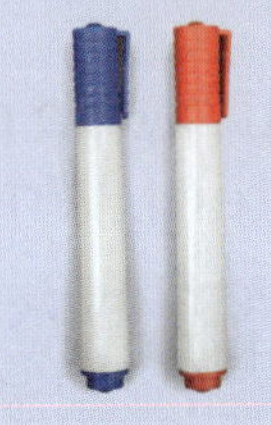

red and blue cellophane

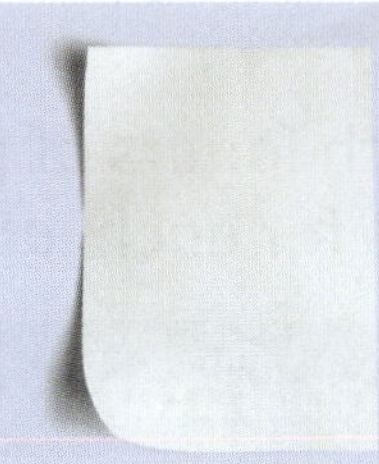

red and blue pencils or markers

paper

tools: ruler, craft knife or scissors, glue, sticky tape

1 Cut out the front frame for your 3D glasses. Use your head dimensions from Unit 22.

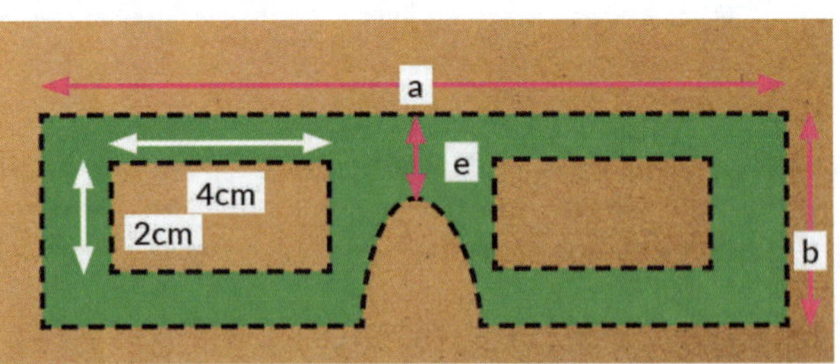

2 Cut out two rectangles for the filters.

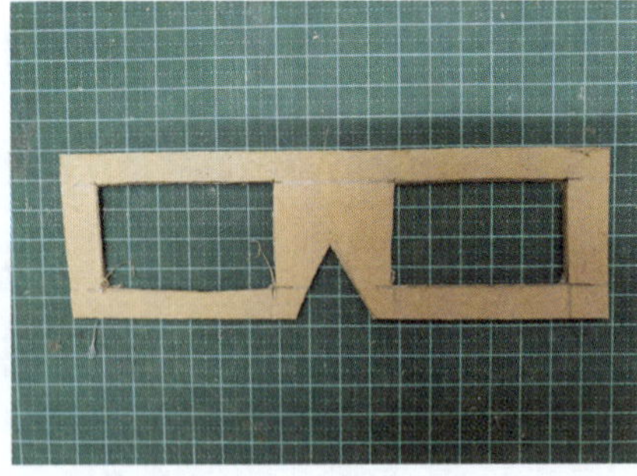

3 Glue or tape red cellophane over one hole and blue over the other.

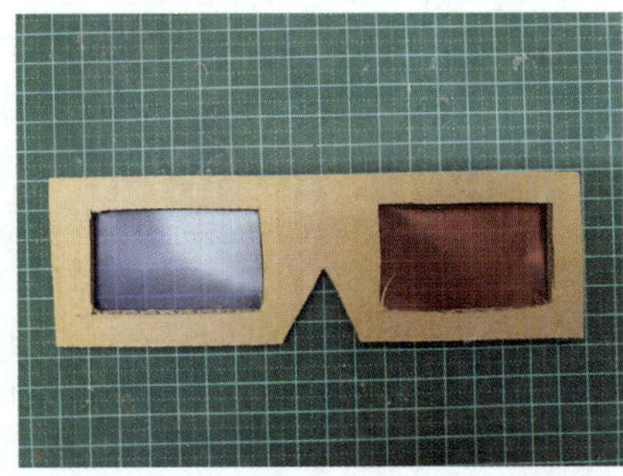

4 Test your glasses with the pictures on the page.

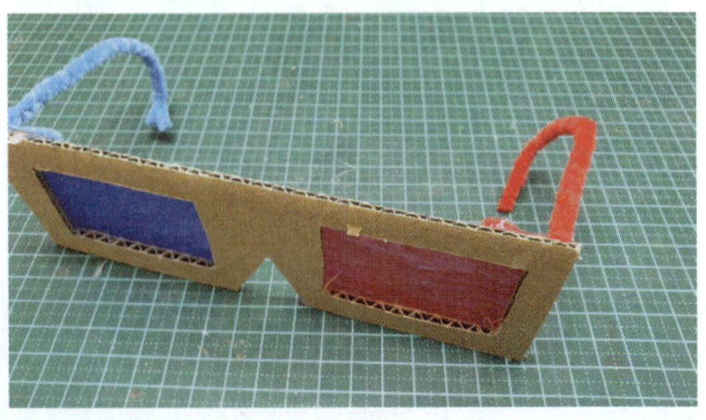

MATHEMATICS

TARGETING STEM JOURNAL 5 @ PASCAL PRESS ISBN 978-1-925726-10-7

1 a Test looking through the glasses with first the red filter on the right eye. Then test them with the red filter on the left eye. Which way is best?

Red on right eye, blue on left	Red on left eye, blue on right

b What do you see if you close one eye? Explain below.

Looking JUST through the red filter	Looking JUST through the blue filter

c Look at the colour bar below using one filter at a time. Describe what you see for each colour.

Red filter								
Blue filter								

2 Draw your own 3D picture on a piece of paper. Draw an outline in blue. Repeat in red, just a little to the side.

3 Do anaglyph glasses have to have red and blue filters? Experiment with other colours of cellophane and record what happens.

Test pictures

The magical refracting pencil

How can we make a magic show using refraction?

When light passes from air to water and from the water back to the air, it bends or refracts.

What you need

two pencils

glass of water

1 Place a pencil behind an empty glass of water. Record what you see. (Journal 1A)

2 Fill the glass with water and repeat. Record what you see. (Journal 1B)

3 Test and record your observations of positions 1C–1E.

4 Try other positions or other items such as your finger and record in 1F–1H.

TARGETING STEM JOURNAL 5 @ PASCAL PRESS ISBN 978-1-925726-10-7

1 Record your observations of the pencil below.

2 Look at the picture. The magician has seen the perfect fish for his magic act. He intends to snatch it from the water. But because of refraction, the fish isn't where his brain thinks it is.

a Is the fish further away, closer or the same distance from where his brain thinks it is? ________________

b Is the fish at the same depth, deeper or shallower than from where his brain thinks it is? ________________

c Complete this sentence with the words *brain, direction, light rays, straight line*.

________________ change ________________ when they travel from water to air but our ____________________ assumes they have travelled in a ____________________

3 Create a mini magic-show to perform for younger students.

Suggestions:

- Introduce the pencil, the water, glass (or all three!) as being 'magical'.
- Use a magic 'arrow' or magic wand instead of a pencil.
- Select the best 'illusion' as your finale.
- Finish your show with an explanation of how refraction, not magic, creates the illusion.

Automatic fire sprinkler

How can we make an automatic fire sprinkler?

Fire sprinklers are activated by heat. They contain a red glass bulb with a liquid inside. The liquid expands when it gets hotter and cracks the glass, allowing water to flow through.

What you need

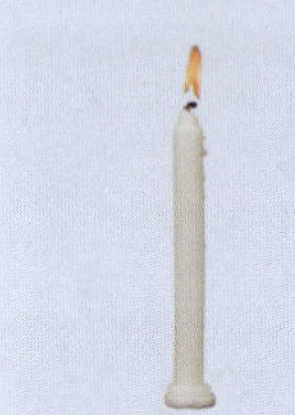

candle and candle wax | small plastic bottle and water | small bucket | 30cm x 15cm corrugated card | tools: scissors, hot glue gun, sticky tape

1 Add half a cup of water to the bottle.

2 Soften some candle wax and then plug the mouth of the bottle.

3 Cut out a hole in the card and push the bottle through. Secure with hot glue or tape.

4 Place the candle in the bottom of the bucket. Complete Journal 1.

1 a Predict what will happen when you light the candle.

____

b Read the Warning section.

c Take it outside in a safe area.

d Observe and record below what happens when you light the candle.

Time	Candle	Wax stopper	Water
0			

2 Did your fire extinguisher work as planned? Why or why not? If not, what do you need to change?

____

____

3 Commercial automatic fire sprinklers are designed to meet specific needs. On a rating of 1–5, consider how suitable your model is for:

Needs	Commercial system	Your system
Putting out large fires	1 2 3 4 5	1 2 3 4 5
Automatically refilling with water	1 2 3 4 5	1 2 3 4 5
Mounting on the ceiling	1 2 3 4 5	1 2 3 4 5
Detecting heat from a distance	1 2 3 4 5	1 2 3 4 5
Being cheap to make	1 2 3 4 5	1 2 3 4 5

DID YOU KNOW?

- An American named Henry S. Parmelee filed patents for automatic fire extinguishers in the 1870s.
- Fire sprinklers are also called fire suppression systems.

- Take care lighting and extinguishing the candle.
- Don't put the flame too close to the plastic bottle.
- Only do this under adult supervision.

TARGETING STEM JOURNAL 5 @ PASCAL PRESS ISBN 978-1-925726-10-7

Kitchen apron design

SCIENCE SSU074, SSU076, SIS065

What you need

a teddy bear, doll or similar toy

paper, plastic or fabric

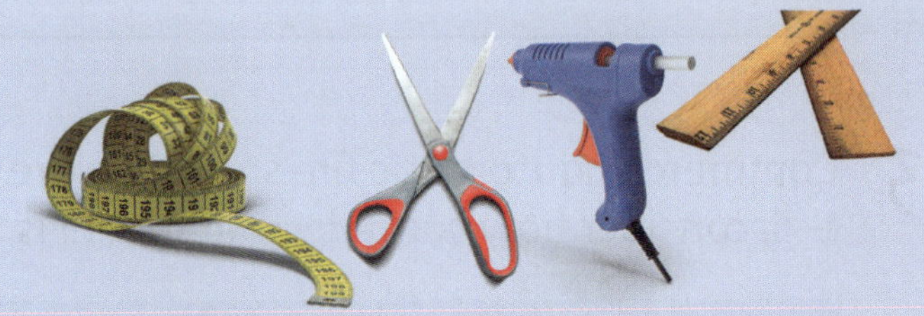
tools: tape measure, ruler, scissors, hot glue gun

1 Complete Journal Step 1. Measure the toy and complete Journal 2.

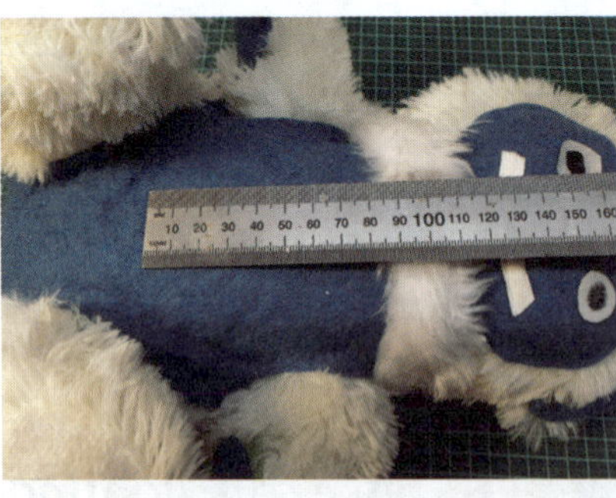

2 Use the diagram to measure out your design on your chosen material.

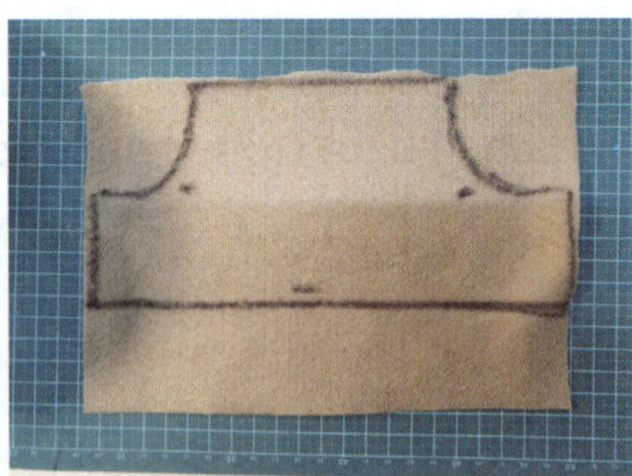

3 Cut out the apron and test fit onto your toy.

4 Cut ties from the same material and attach at the top and sides.

MATHEMATICS MMG084

TARGETING STEM JOURNAL 5 @ PASCAL PRESS ISBN 978-1-925726-10-7

1 a Read the Design Brief then decide which material will best meet the requirements.

	Paper	Plastic	Cloth	Required?
Ease of construction	Easy <---> Difficult	Easy <---> Difficult	Easy <---> Difficult	☐
Recyclable	Yes No	Yes No	Yes No	☐
Washable	Yes No	Yes No	Yes No	☐
Waterproof	Yes No	Yes No	Yes No	☐
Cost	Low <---> High	Low <---> High	Low <---> High	☐
Strength	Weak <---> Strong	Weak <---> Strong	Weak <---> Strong	☐
Visual appeal	Low <---> High	Low <---> High	Low <---> High	☐
Can include pocket	Yes No	Yes No	Yes No	☐

b Explain what material you will use for the apron and why it meets the design brief the best.

___

2 Measure the toy using the guide at the bottom.

	Toy	Person
1 Collar to knees		
2 Inside arm to inside arm		
3 Collar to waist		
4 Around the hips		

3 Using the same steps as above, design an apron for yourself or a friend.

Design Brief

'Bears 'R' Us' is producing a new range of 'kid & kitchen friendly' teddy bears. They need a range of aprons to go with the bears that are washable, colourful and strong. The aprons also need to keep the bears' expensive fur protected in dusty and wet kitchens and must include at least one pocket.

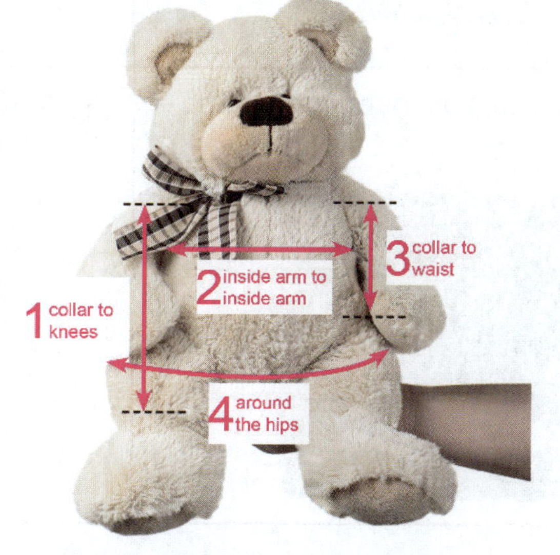

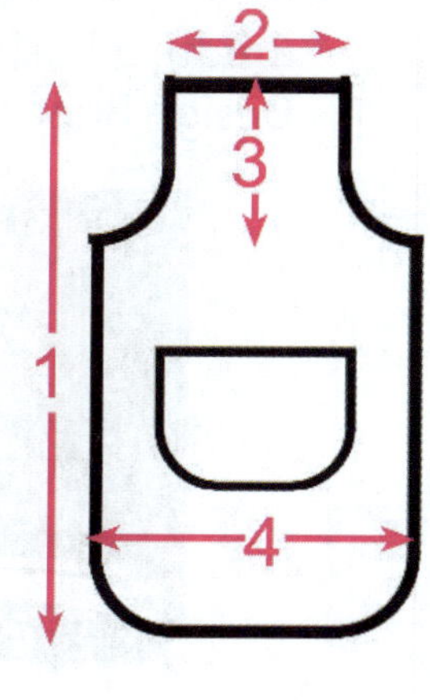

TARGETING STEM JOURNAL 5 @ PASCAL PRESS ISBN 978-1-925726-10-7

Outdoor musical instruments

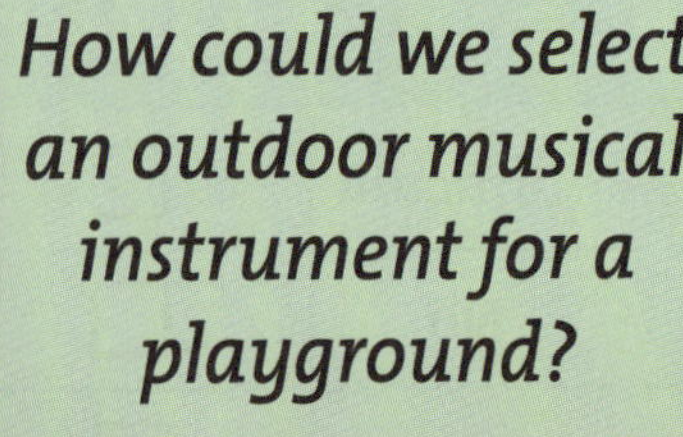
How could we select an outdoor musical instrument for a playground?

Playground equipment needs to be appealing to children, safe to use and not too expensive. It also needs to be accessible to disabled people, not easily broken and preferably made from recycled and sustainable materials.

What you need

card

modelling materials

sand, small rocks, wood

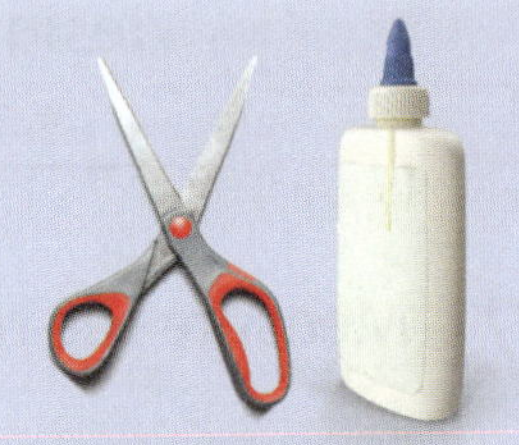
tools: scissors, glue, paint

1 Complete Journal 1. Sketch out a plan.

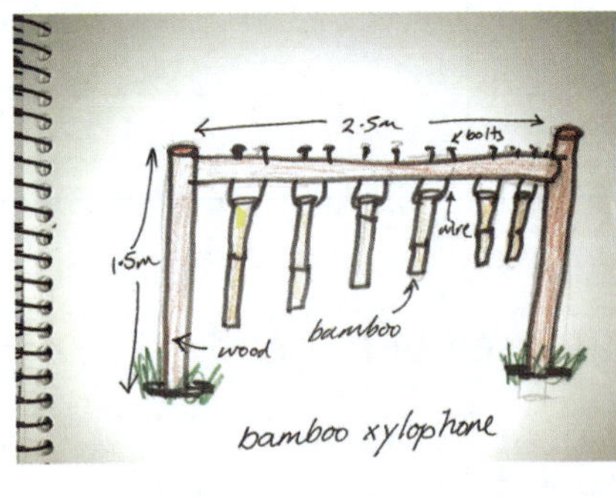

2 Make a model of the musical instrument.

3 Create a bush setting as mentioned in the Design Brief.

4 Add models of children playing your instrument. Display with your proposal.

1 a Read the Yidaki Playground Design Brief below. Use the information to assess how each instrument would meet their requirements.

Criteria	Bongo drums	Beach xylophone	Tubular bells
Details	Commercial product. Search 'rainbow-trio-bongos'.	Homemade. Different length branches threaded on wire between trees.	Homemade. Stainless steel tubing cut to length and mounted on frame. Search for costs in your area.
Practical Considerations			
Appeal	Attractive | Plain | Unattractive	Attractive | Plain | Unattractive	Attractive | Plain | Unattractive
Cost	<$100 | $100 - $1000 | >$1000	<$100 | $100 - $1000 | >$1000	<$100 | $100 - $1000 | >$1000
Installation	DIY | Adults | Professional	DIY | Adults | Professional	DIY | Adults | Professional
Accessories	Hands | Beaters	Hands | Beaters	Hands | Beaters
Strength	High | Medium | Low	High | Medium | Low	High | Medium | Low
People Access	Non-disabled only | All people	Non-disabled only | All people	Non-disabled only | All people
Sustainability Considerations			
Renewable Materials	None | Some | All	None | Some | All	None | Some | All
Safety Risks	Very safe |Safe | Unsafe	Very safe |Safe | Unsafe	Very safe |Safe | Unsafe
Can be recycled	None | Some | All	None | Some | All	None | Some | All
Other			

b Write your recommendation on which instrument to put up in the playground with reasons why.

____

____

Yidaki Playground Design Brief

The local council is considering a request for some outdoor musical instruments for the Yidaki children's playground. They want an attractive and playable instrument that would fit into the natural bush setting. Lots of families with young children and old grandparents visit, so it needs to be both robust and safe. Their budget is $2000.

Night into day

How much light does it take to turn off a solar-powered light?

Solar-powered lights turn on when it is dark and off when it is light. They do this when a sensor, called a photoreceptor, detects that it is dark or light.

What you need

dark room

bright torch

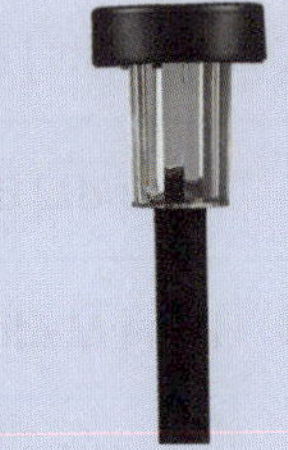

garden solar light

1 Make sure the solar light is fully charged, then test the light in a dark room to check it turns on.

2 Shine the torch at the solar light. Try different directions and angles until the solar light turns off.

3 Locate the photoreceptor and complete Journal 1.

4 Read through Journal 2 and test for light intensity.

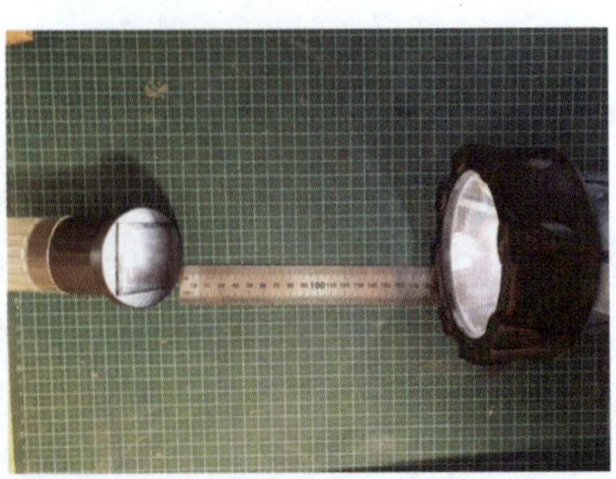

TARGETING STEM JOURNAL 5 @ PASCAL PRESS ISBN 978-1-925726-10-7

1 Draw a solar light below and label it: solar cell, photoreceptor, protective glass, lamp cover, LED.

2 The further the torch light is away from the photoreceptor, the weaker or less intense its beam is. Complete the table to show how close you must be for the torch to turn off the solar light.

Distance from photoreceptor	Solar light off	Solar light on
0cm		
10cm		
20cm		

3 Take your solar light outside. Can you make it turn on in the day? Explain what you did.

4 Should light installation manuals include recommendations to avoid placing solar lights near other bright lights such as streetlights, house windows or floodlights? Why or why not?

DID YOU KNOW?

Solar power was discovered by Alexandre Edmond Becquerel in 1839 when he showed you could generate electricity directly from sunlight.

The International Space Station has 84KW of solar panels.

Around 300,000km^2 of solar panels would supply the world's energy needs. That's around the combined area of New Zealand and Tasmania.

Make the switch

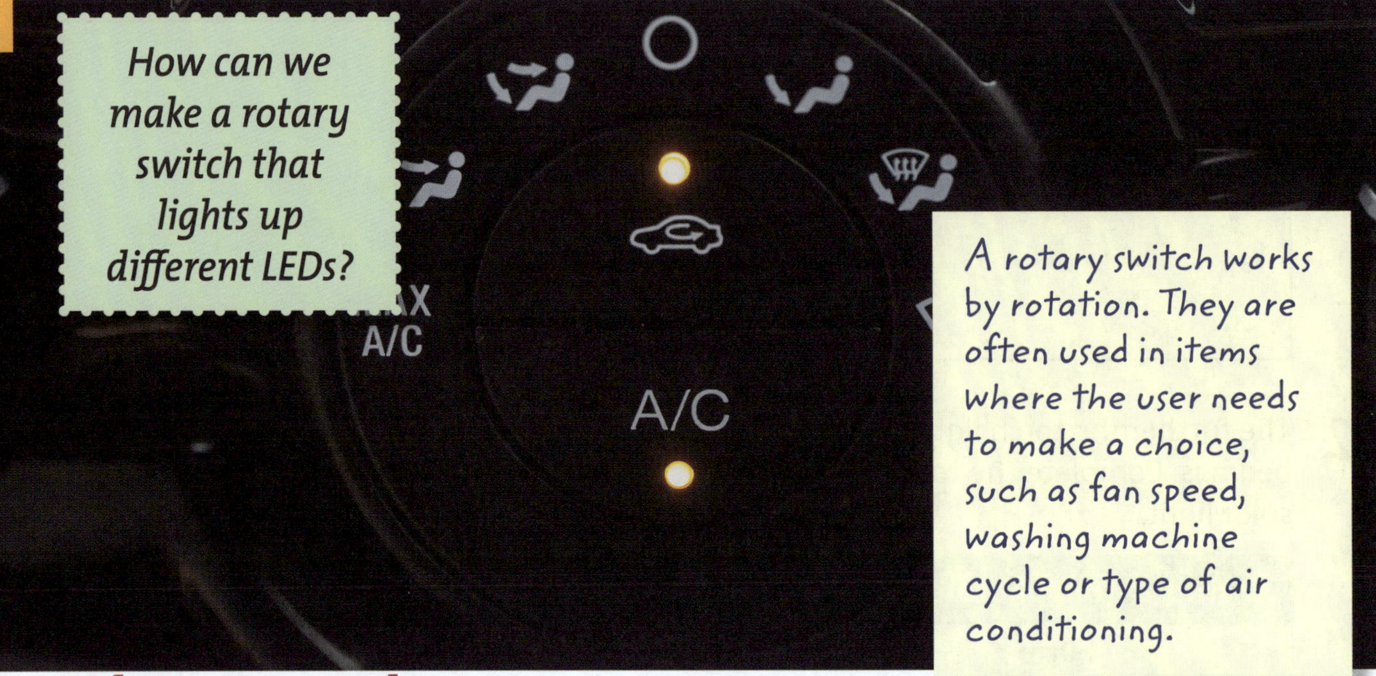

How can we make a rotary switch that lights up different LEDs?

A rotary switch works by rotation. They are often used in items where the user needs to make a choice, such as fan speed, washing machine cycle or type of air conditioning.

What you need

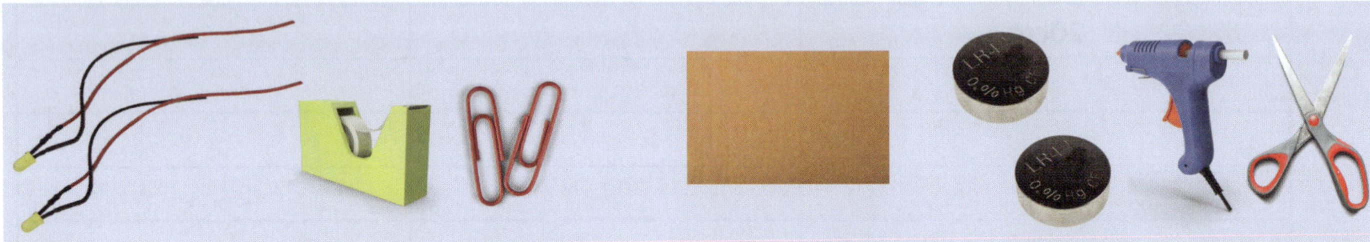

2 LEDs | tape, paper fastener, paperclips, bulldog clip and wire | corrugated cardboard or plastic-board | two 1½V button batteries | tools: hot glue gun, scissors

1 Make the battery pack (Journal 1) and LED switch card (Journal 2).

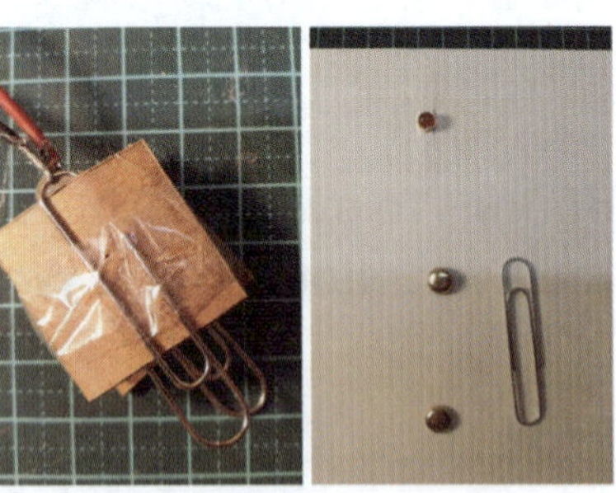

2 On the front of the card, slide a paperclip under the centre split pin.

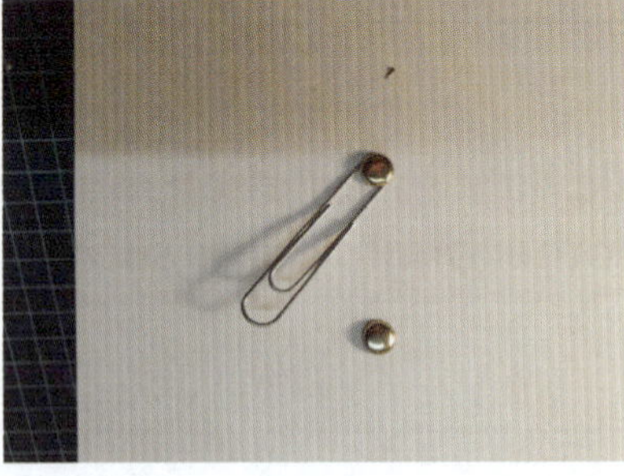

3 Test your switch.

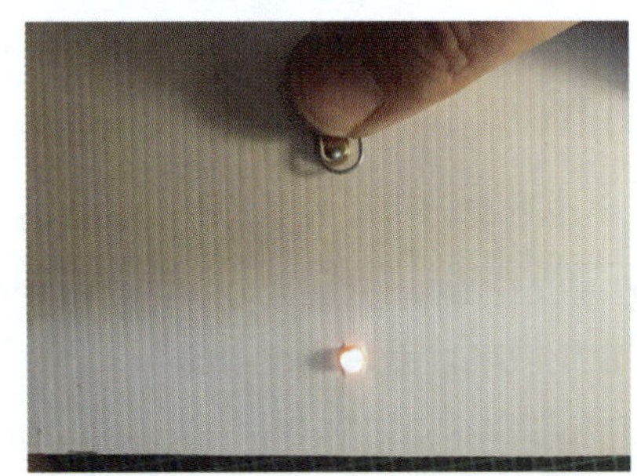

4 Use the ideas in Journal 3 to make a rotary switch that can light up different LEDs.

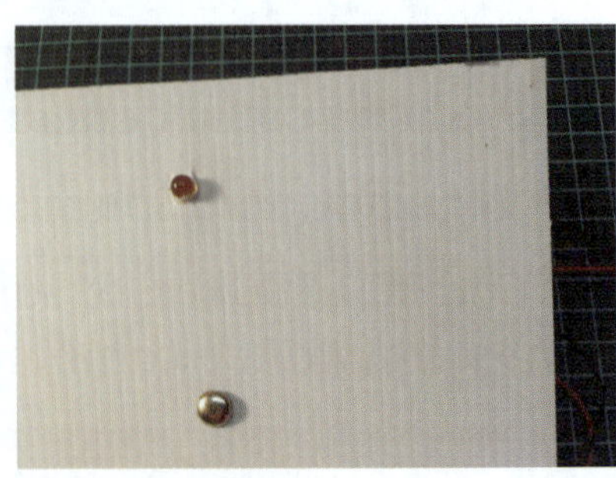

TARGETING STEM JOURNAL 5 @ PASCAL PRESS ISBN 978-1-925726-10-7

1 Make the battery holder:

a Cut out two 3cm squares of card.

b Attach 10cm of wire to each of two paperclips.

c Slide the paperclips onto the edge of the squares and hot glue in place.

d Stack the batteries side by side (plus to minus) and place between the two cards. Tape together and mark the positive and negative sides.

2 Make the LED switch card:

a Push two paper fasteners through the card, about one paperclip distance apart. Make a hole and push the LED through.

b Bend down its longer (positive) lead and secure under a paper fastener.

c Bend down the shorter (negative lead) and attach it to the battery pack's negative wire.

d Attach the positive battery wire to the second split pin.

3 Adapt the board so it can light up one or more additional LEDs. Draw your idea on page below then build and test it. Suggestions:

- Add another paper fastener pin and LED.
- The shorter (negative) lead of the LED should join to the first LED's shorter lead.
- Position extra paper fasteners in a semi-circle from the centre.

DEFINITIONS

The long lead on a LED is called the anode and is positive.

The short lead on a LED is called the cathode and is negative.

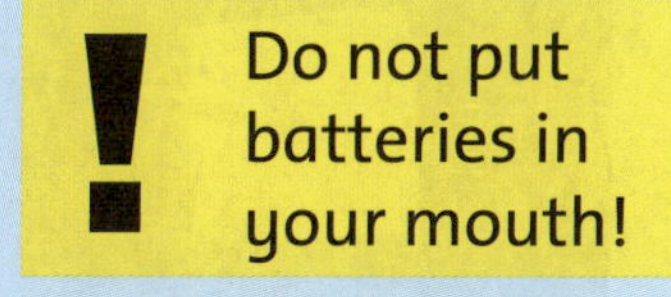

Be alarmed

How can we make an alarm that shows when a door is opened?

An emergency exit door will set off alarms when opened from inside. As well as alerting people to danger, it also alerts against unauthorised use of the door.

What you need

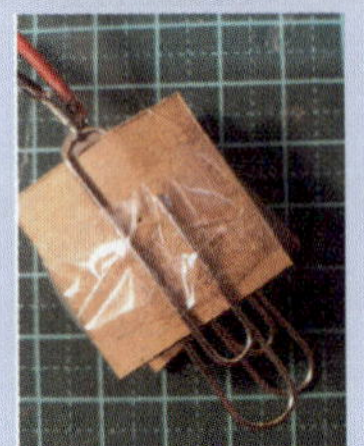

battery pack from Unit 29

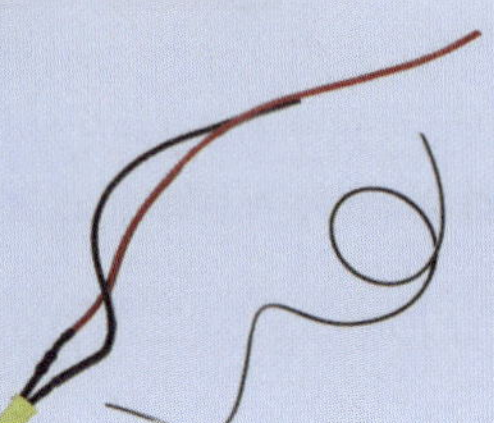

LED, wire

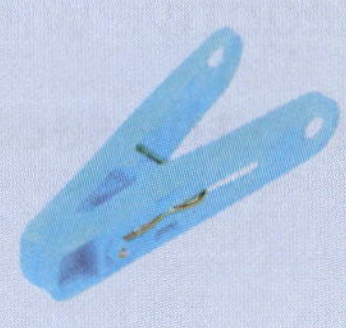

clothes peg

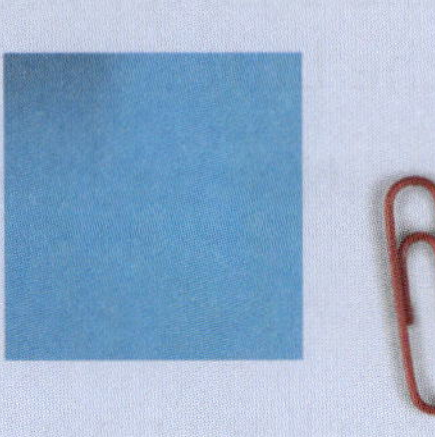

string, plastic container, card, paperclips

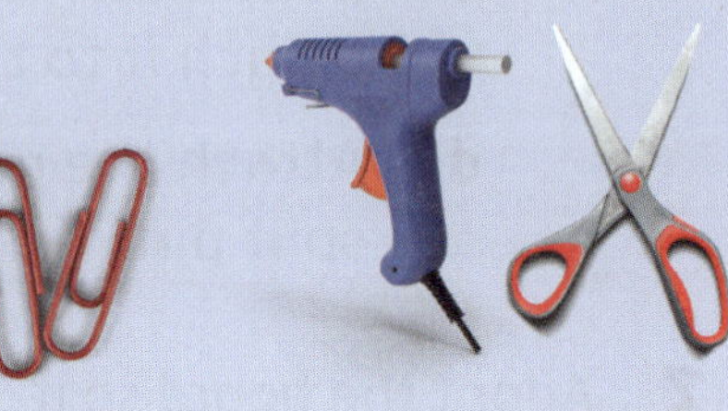

tools: hot glue gun, scissors

1 Attach 10cm of wire to each of two paperclips.

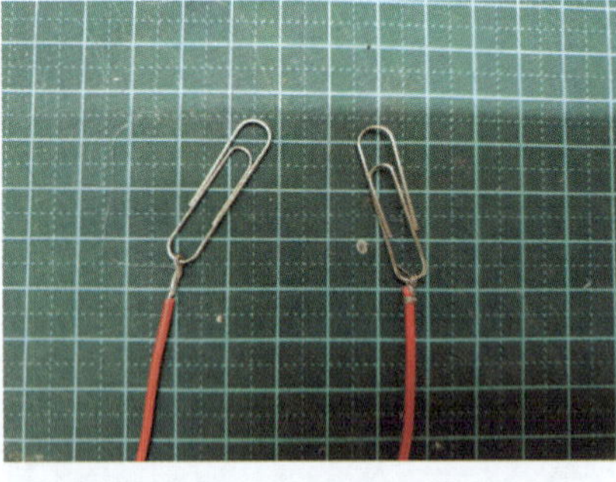

2 Slide the paperclips onto the 'jaw' ends of the peg. Hot glue the paperclips on the outside of the jaws.

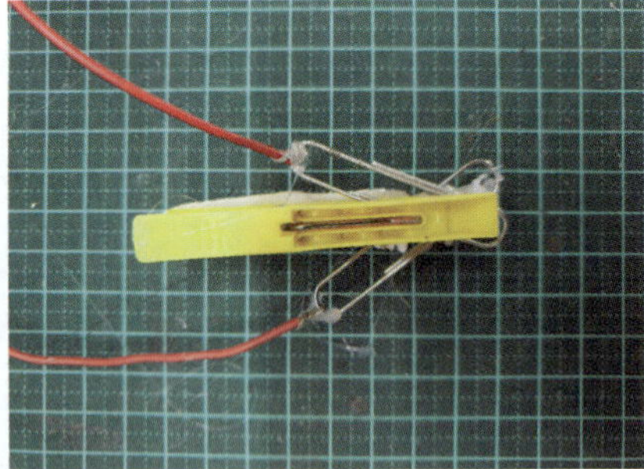

3 Cut a 2cm square from the plastic container. Use a nail to push a hole through near the edge.

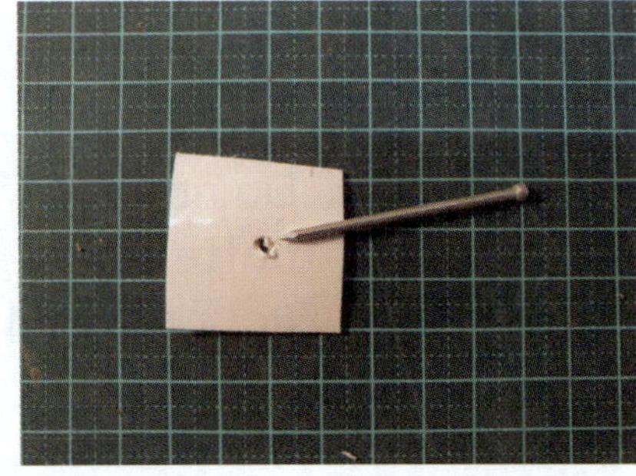

4 Tie the string to the hole. Place the plastic square in the peg's jaws.

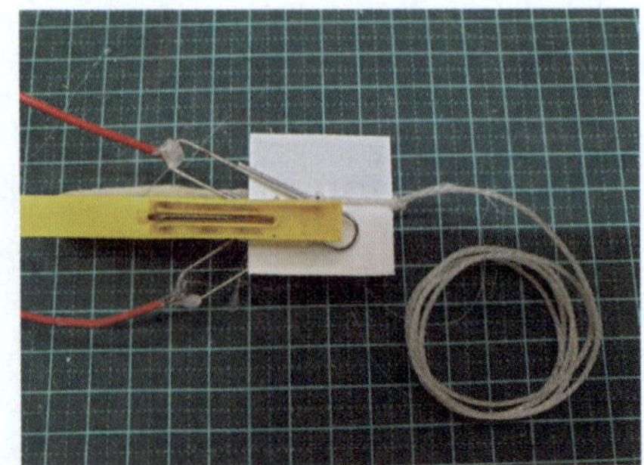

TARGETING STEM JOURNAL 5 @ PASCAL PRESS ISBN 978-1-925726-10-7

1 Assemble the alarm switch.

a Push the LED into the board and glue the peg near the side.

b Attach the negative battery pack wire to the LED's shorter (negative) lead.

c Attach one wire from the peg to the LED's longer (positive) lead.

d Attach the peg's other wire to the LED's other lead.

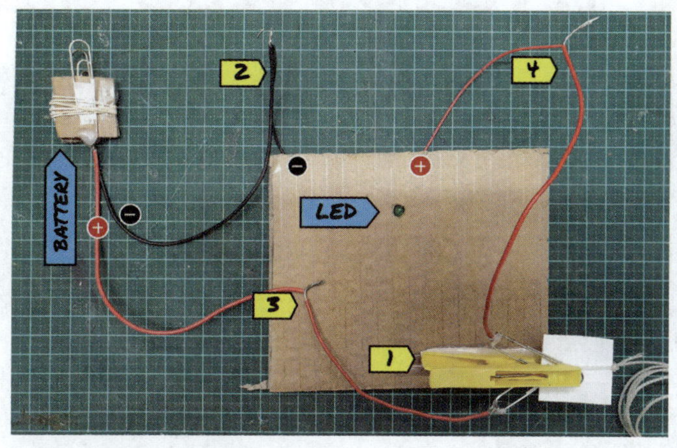

2 Test your switch by gently pulling the plastic out.

a Explain what happens.

____

b If necessary, troubleshoot your switch. You may need to:

- Adjust the pressure of the peg jaws by not allowing them to fully close.
- Secure the peg more firmly with a bulldog clip or tape.
- Attach the string more firmly to the plastic square.

3 Attach your alarm switch to a door or other moveable object. Explain in words and pictures below what you did and how well it worked.

____

____

____

Be careful around doors, especially where people may not see you working.

Hydroponic garden

How well can plants grow without soil?

Hydroponic plants are grown in liquid nutrients rather than soil. Hydroponic systems use less water than conventional farming but are more expensive to set up.

What you need

2L plastic bottle | cotton cloth | lettuce or spinach seeds | coconut fibre (hanging basket liner) | soluble hydroponic fertiliser | tools: craft knife, scissors | pot with soil (Journal 1)

1 Cut the neck off the bottle. Push a 20cm cloth strip into the hole.

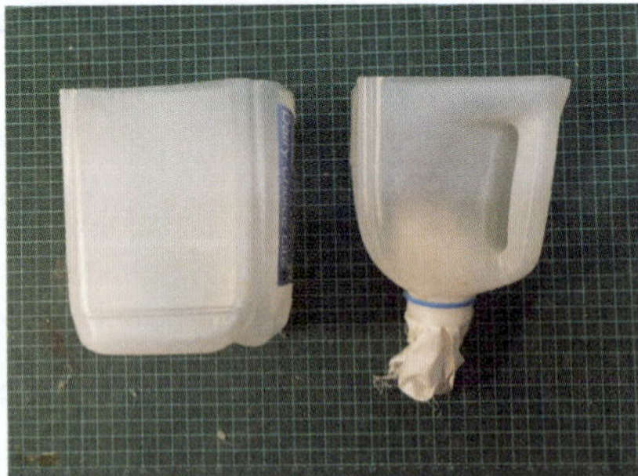

2 Mix and add the fertiliser to the bottle. (See Warning)

3 Line the neck with damp coconut fibre.

4 Place 3-4 seeds in the centre of the coconut fibre and cover.

TARGETING STEM JOURNAL 5 @ PASCAL PRESS ISBN 978-1-925726-10-7

1 **a** Plant the same number of seeds into a small pot of soil. Place both systems in a sunny place, such as a window sill or bench near a window.

b Observe how the two sets of plants grow. Record when they germinate, their growth, when you watered them, added more nutrients or weeded.

Date	Hydroponic Plant	Soil Plant

2 After a month, answer these questions:

a How many seeds germinated? ____________________

b Which system produced the most / best plants? ____________________

c Which system required the most work to maintain? ____________________

3 What advantages and disadvantages are there to growing plants hydroponically? Think about: cost, weeds, pests, harvesting, sustainability, space and fertiliser.

Advantages	Disadvantages

DID YOU KNOW?

The word *hydroponics* comes from the words *hydro* (meaning 'water') and *ponos* (meaning 'work').

Hydroponics is used to grow fresh food on the International Space Station.

Adult supervision is required for mixing the hydroponic fertiliser.

TARGETING STEM JOURNAL 5 @ PASCAL PRESS ISBN 978-1-925726-10-7

Colourful dyes

How can we add colours to textiles using natural dyes and a hammer?

Dyeing is the process of adding colour to fibres. Natural dyes are sourced from plants, minerals and even insects. Synthetic dyes are manufactured from chemicals.

What you need

white cotton squares | flowers | newspaper, baking paper | tools: hammer, safety goggles

1 Remove the stems from the flowers.

2 Place the newspaper on a strong surface. Place the baking paper on top.

3 Arrange the flowers on the cloth then cover with baking paper.

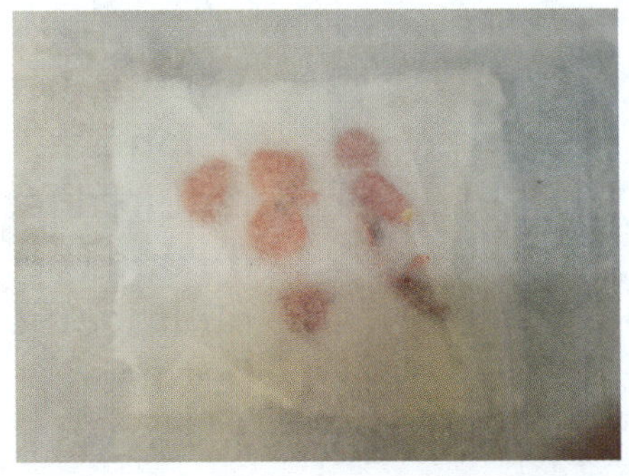

4 Hammer the flowers through the paper.

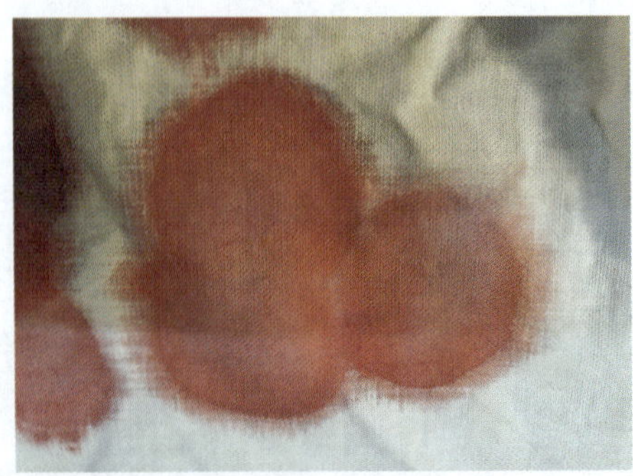

TARGETING STEM JOURNAL 5 @ PASCAL PRESS ISBN 978-1-925726-10-7

1 Repeat the process but with smaller pieces of material. Experiment to see how best to preserve the designs so that the dye doesn't rub off. Explain what happens if you:

a Soak in warm water ______________________________

b Soak in cold water ______________________________

c Iron over the design ______________________________

2 Look at the flow chart below. It shows how textiles are produced, starting with growing the fibres.

At what stage (a, b, c or d) do you think the *dyeing* is carried out? Give reasons for your answer.

____

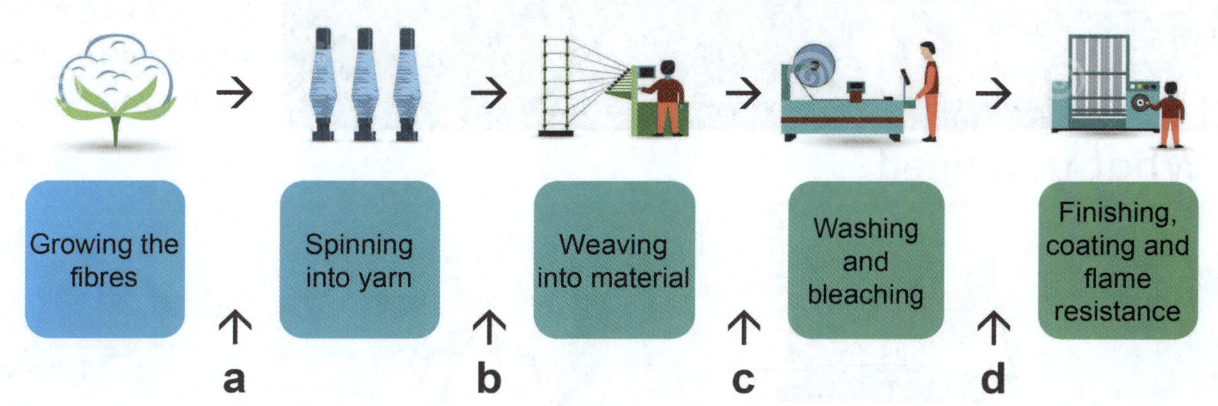

3 Are natural dyes better for the environment than synthetic dyes? There are positives and negatives on both sides. Read the article 'Dye Off: Natural vs Synthetic' *(tdsblog.com/dye-off-natural-vs-synthetic)*.

DID YOU KNOW?

Large amounts of water are used at every stage of the textile production process. One estimate is that it takes 2,700 litres to produce a cotton t-shirt.

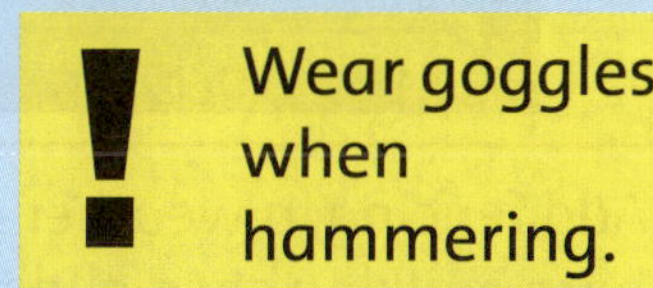

Purple dye was once called 'Tyrian Purple' made from a snail. It became so rare it was worth its weight in gold!

Our highland goats

How can we start a goat farm on the school oval?

To raise funds, your school has decided to turn the oval into a goat farm. You have been asked to make a model showing fencing, buildings and a flock size estimate based on the size of your oval.

What you need

large card

craft materials

tools: hot glue gun, scissors, ruler

tape measure or trundle wheel (Journal 1)

1 Complete Journal 1. Draw out your rough plan to scale on a sheet of card.

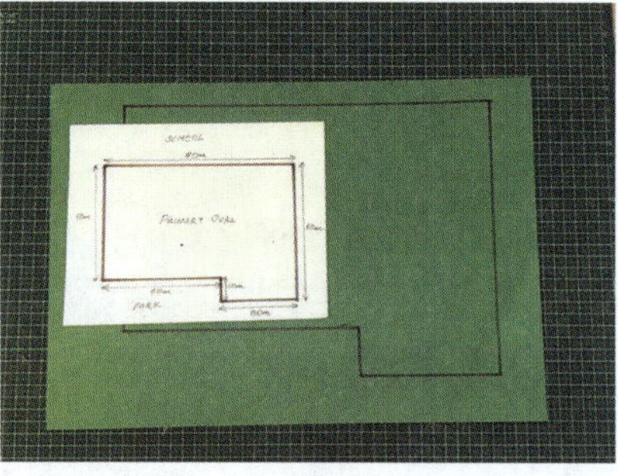

2 Complete Journal 2. Make a herd of small goat models from the modelling clay.

3 Add fencing, a weather shelter, sleeping barn, milking shed and feeding troughs.

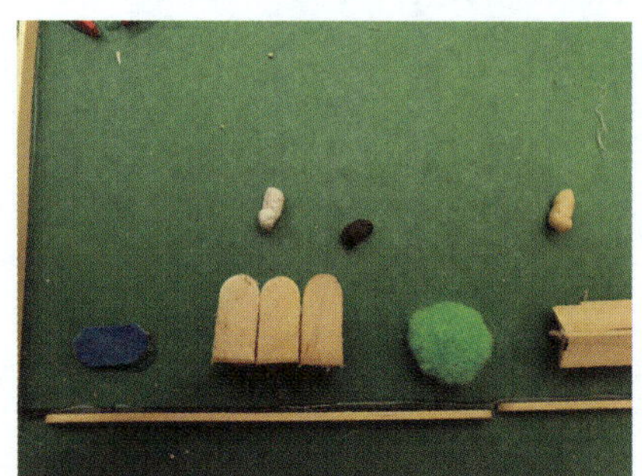

4 Complete Journal 3 and 4. Write out your conclusions and attach them to the finished model.

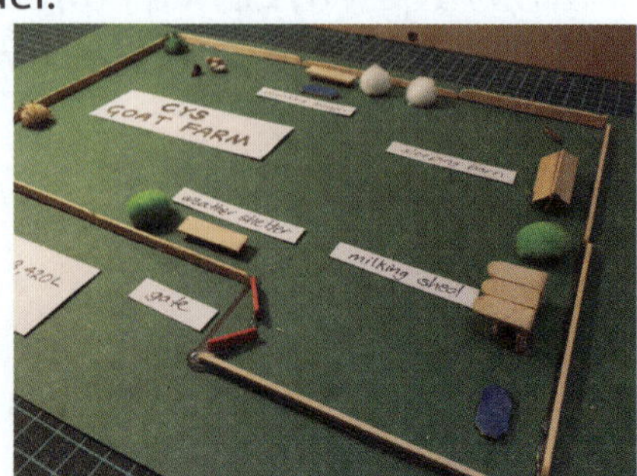

TARGETING STEM JOURNAL 5 @ PASCAL PRESS ISBN 978-1-925726-10-7

1 Map: Draw a map of the school oval below. Add measurements so you can calculate its area.

a Our school oval is _______________ m^2

b Divide by 10,000 to calculate its area in hectares. _______________ ha

2 Number of goats. The maximum number of animals you should have on a farm is called its Carrying Capacity. This is usually calculated using the farm's rainfall, area and type of animal. Most schools, though, are in suburban areas and must follow local council rules. Use the information below to calculate the number of goats allowed on your oval based on a typical council allowance of six goats for each hectare.

Your oval area in hectares (1b) ×	6 goats / hectare =	Number of goats

3 Calculate how much money selling goat milk will raise. The example below is for a Saanen goat which averages 3.8 litres a day over 10 months/year of milk production.

Number of goats ×	Litres per day ×	10 months ×	Price per litre =	Total for year

4 **a** List additional requirements below and look online to find approximate costs. For example, fencing would cost around $840 for each 100m. Goats would cost between $100 and $3000 depending on their breed. The goats would also need a barn, a milking shed and water troughs.

____

____

____

b Is this project a good way to raise money? Why or why not?

____

Dish-washer vs dishwasher

Does washing by hand use more water or less water than a dishwasher?

Any system of washing dishes requires water, energy to heat the water, chemicals to assist with removing dirt and scraps and either human energy or electricity for scrubbing.

What you need

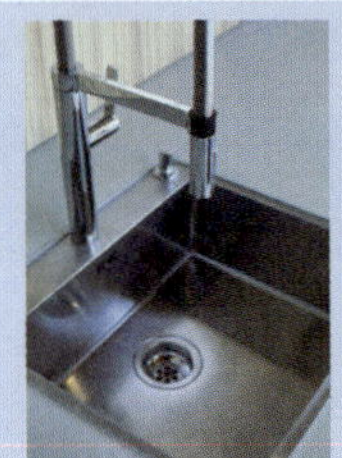
a sink

a four-place setting of plates, dishes, cups, saucers and cutlery

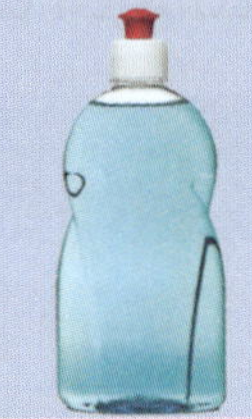
dishwashing liquid

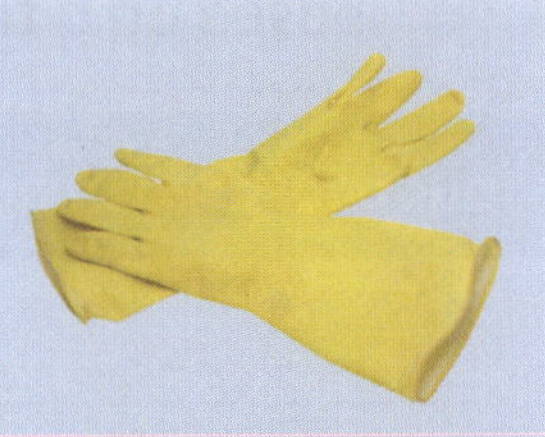
rubber gloves

1 Complete Journal 1 and calculate the flow of water from your tap.

2 'Soil' your setting by getting it dirty. For example, use them for lunch!

3 Wash them under running water and record the time in Journal 2 OR

4 Fill a sink to wash them and calculate how much water you used in Journal 2.

TARGETING STEM JOURNAL 5 @ PASCAL PRESS ISBN 978-1-925726-10-7

1 Calculate the **flow rate** from your selected tap.

a. Turn your tap onto a medium flow.

b. Time how long it takes to fill a litre jug to the top. ____________ seconds.

c. Divide 60 by the time in (b) and calculate the **flow rate.**

$$\frac{60}{\text{Time to fill a one litre jug}} = \text{____ litres/min}$$

2 Calculate how much water your handwashing system used:

Multiply the time the tap was running by the flow rate of the tap.

Time tap was running x Flow rate = Amount of water used

3 Look at this information from an Australian dishwasher.

Program	Degree of soil	Type of load	Program phases	Duration (min)	Energy (kWhh)	Water (litres)
ECO 50°	Normal	Crockery & Cutlery	• Prewash • Wash 50°C • Rinse and dry	129	0.75	11.6L

a. How much water does the dishwasher system use? ____________

b. How much water did your system use? ____________

c. Most dishwashers can wash an eight-place setting. How long would it take the handwashing system to wash **twice as much** crockery and cutlery? ____________

d. Based on your test and the information above, which system of washing dishes uses the **least** amount of water? ____________

____

4 Our test only looked at which system used the least amount of water. What other advantages do the two systems have?

Hand-washing system	Dishwasher system

A little free library

How can we make a Little Free Library for students in your class?

'Little Free Library' is a worldwide system of lending books in the local community. It features miniature library enclosures made from recycled materials and a lending system of 'take one – leave one'.

What you need

old children's books

a sturdy cardboard box

art supplies

1 Make shelves in your box for different sized books.

2 Add a door and roof to make an interesting 'library'.

3 Decorate your Little Free Library. Add a 'take one – leave one' sign.

4 Fill with old books.

TARGETING STEM JOURNAL 5 @ PASCAL PRESS ISBN 978-1-925726-10-7

1 Here are some suggestions for a location for your Little Free Library (LFL). What advantages and disadvantages does each have? For example, is vandalism a problem? Is rain? Can you easily refill it? Who do you have to get permission from?

Location	Advantages	Disadvantages
Classroom		
Corridor		
Playground		
Admin office		

2 Set up your LFL in your preferred location. Keep a record of how lending goes over a week.

Day	Books borrowed	New books lent	Notes
Monday			
Tuesday			
Wednesday			
Thursday			
Friday			

3 How can tell if your LFL is a success? Decide on your criteria and write it below.

___

4 If your LFL is popular, it can be hard to keep track of books in and out. What process could you put in place to tell if a book is a new one or an old one? Think about how big libraries keep track of books. Write your idea below.

___

___

5 Did you have any problems with your LFL? List them below and decide how they could be solved.

Problem	Solution
Some books aren't borrowed.	**Change them for more interesting books.**

Forks vs chopsticks

What is the most efficient utensil for eating food?

The invention of both forks and chopsticks can be traced back to ancient China.

What you need

a fork | chopsticks | two bowls | a variety of different foods (see Journal 1)

1 Read Journal 1 and write in the foods you have access to.

2 Set up two bowls 50cm apart.

3 Time and record how much of each food you can successfully transfer from one bowl to another in 30 seconds using the chopsticks.

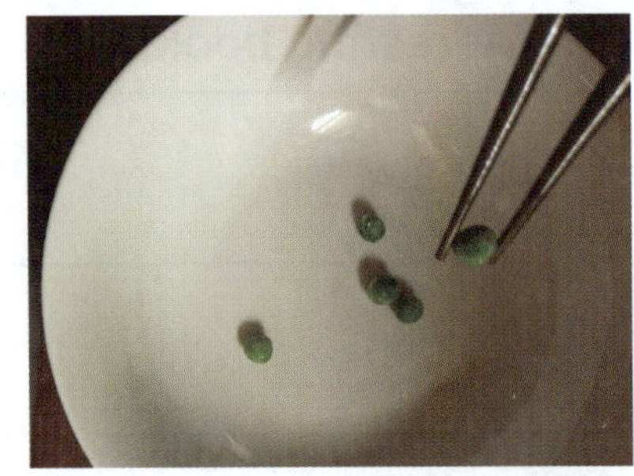

4 Repeat using the fork.

TARGETING STEM JOURNAL 5 @ PASCAL PRESS ISBN 978-1-925726-10-7

1 Choose some foods to test such as popcorn, ice cubes, M&Ms, peas, or beans. Write them below. Time the quantity of each food that can be moved from one bowl to another in 30 seconds.

Food	Chopsticks	Fork	Notes
Ice cubes			

2 a. Was this a fair test? Why or why not?

____

b. What foods would be difficult to eat with chopsticks?

____

c. What foods would be difficult to eat with a fork?

____

d. Based on your results and your answers above, which eating utensil would you find more efficient? ______________________________

____

3 How do forks and chopsticks compare in sustainability? Complete the chart below. You may need to research some criteria.

	Chopsticks	Forks
Are made from sustainable materials		
Can be recycled		
Can be hygienically cleaned		
Can be reused multiple times		

4 What advantages and disadvantages would different eating utensils have for astronauts in zero-g? Hint: Think about how gravity helps keep food on a utensil.

____

____

5 A 'spork' is a combination spoon and a fork. Design a combination utensil of your own such a 'chop-spoon' or a 'fork-stick'.

TDEK012, TDEK013, TDEK014, TDEK015, TDEK016, TDEK017

TECH & DESIGN

TARGETING STEM JOURNAL 5 @ PASCAL PRESS ISBN 978-1-925726-10-7

Peripherals mobile

How can we visualise the flow of data between components in a digital sytem?

Keyboards, mice, webcams, monitors, printers and speakers are all peripherals that are connected together through a digital device's central processing unit. Input peripherals transmit data to the CPU while output peripherals receive data and display or store it in some way.

What you need

drawing or photo of a CPU

thick card

thin thread and thick wool

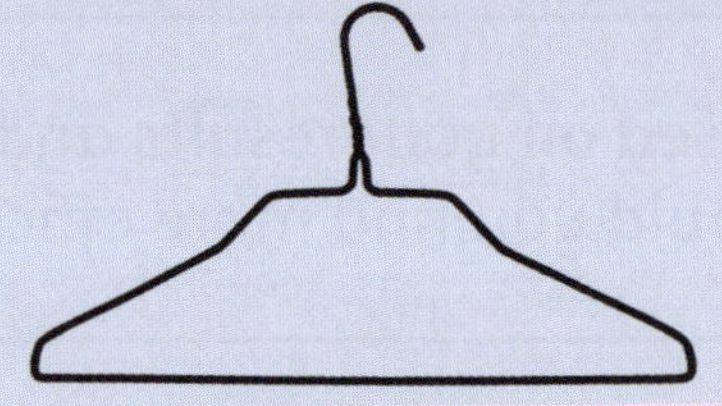
a wire clothes hanger

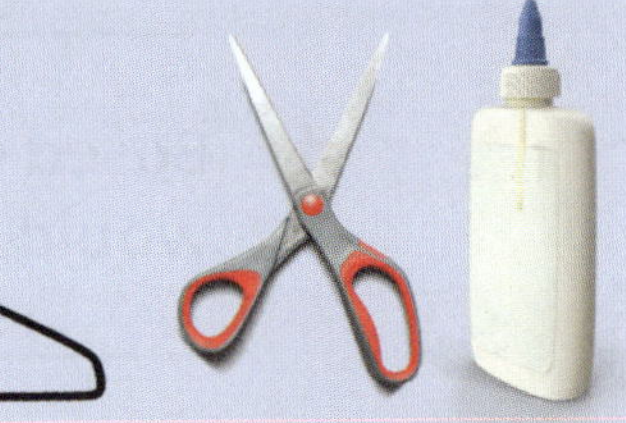
glue and scissors

1 Complete Journal 1 and 2. Mount the photos or drawings of peripherals onto circular pieces of card. Mount the photo or drawing of a CPU onto a rectangular piece of card.

2 Attach the input devices to the clothes hanger with thin thread.

3 Attach the CPU below the input devices with thick wool.

4 Attach the output devices below the CPU with thick wool.

SCIENCE

MATHEMATICS

TARGETING STEM JOURNAL 5 @ PASCAL PRESS ISBN 978-1-925726-10-7

1 Think about the peripherals in the list. Decide if they are for inputting data (like a keyboard) or for outputting data to (like a monitor). Do any peripherals do both? Add other peripherals that you find.

Peripheral	Input device	Output device
Keyboard		
Microphone		
Mouse		
Projector		
Scanner		
Speaker		
Touchpad		
USB Thumb Drive		
Webcam		

2 Choose three input and three output devices. Write your choices below. Find or photograph them and print out 15cm × 15cm pictures. Alternatively, draw them on paper.

My input devices	My output devices

3 Add labels to your mobile that show the flow of data from the input devices to the CPU and from the CPU to the output devices.

4 Some peripherals can both send and receive data from the CPU. For example, external storage devices such as USB drives can send stored data to the CPU and store data sent from the CPU.

Update your mobile with a peripheral that does both. Think about how you will mount it on your mobile and how you will show the two-way data flow.

Cable treasure hunt

Cables, cables everywhere — how many can you find?

Cables are used to connect peripherals such keyboards, monitors and external storage to digital devices with end-connectors that fit specific devices and brands.

What you need

eagle eyes!

assorted cables (See warning.)

1 Look at the cable plugs in the chart in Journal 1.

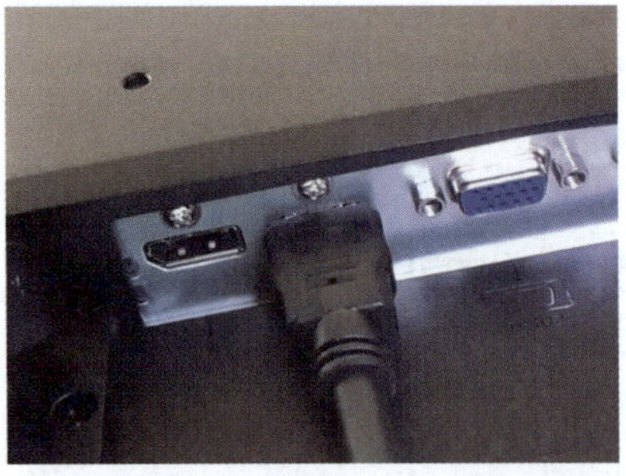

2 Find devices that use those plugs to connect with each other. (See warning.)

3 Record the devices that the cable connects. Decide which way data is flowing.

4 Locate different cables. Draw the plug in the chart and add the information to it.

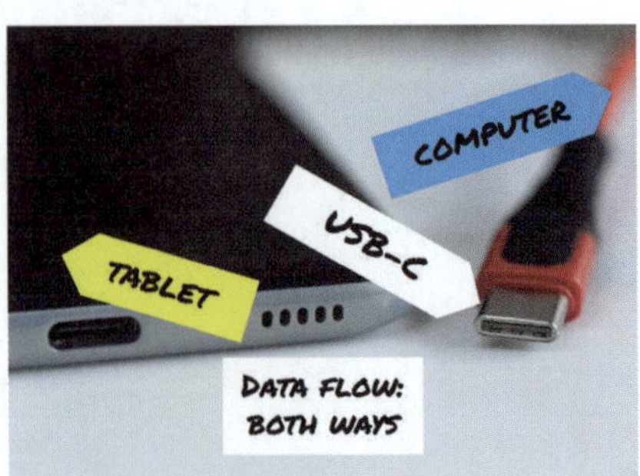

TARGETING STEM JOURNAL 5 @ PASCAL PRESS ISBN 978-1-925726-10-7

Plug	What devices did it connect?	Data flow: In / out / both
	TO	
	Cable name:	
	TO	
	Cable name:	
	TO	
	Cable name:	
	TO	
	Cable name:	
	TO	
	Cable name:	
	TO	
	Cable name:	
	TO	
	Cable name:	
	TO	
	Cable name:	
	TO	
	Cable name:	
	TO	
	Cable name:	
	TO	
	Cable name:	

Do NOT unplug cables to check their plugs without permission! Some peripherals, such as storage devices, can be damaged if they are unplugged incorrectly.

Wi-fi blind spots

Where are the wi-fi blind spots around your school?

Wi-fi signals are radio waves. A 'blind spot' is a place where the radio waves from the wireless router don't reach because it is too far away or the waves have been weakened ('attenuated') by the materials they pass through.

What you need

phone, tablet or other wireless device

wireless signal strength meter app

map of school

1 Measure and record the Wi-fi signal in your classroom.

2 Measure the signal in nearby classrooms.

3 Move outside into the school yard. Find locations with little or no signal.

4 Mark the blind spots on your map. (Journal 2)

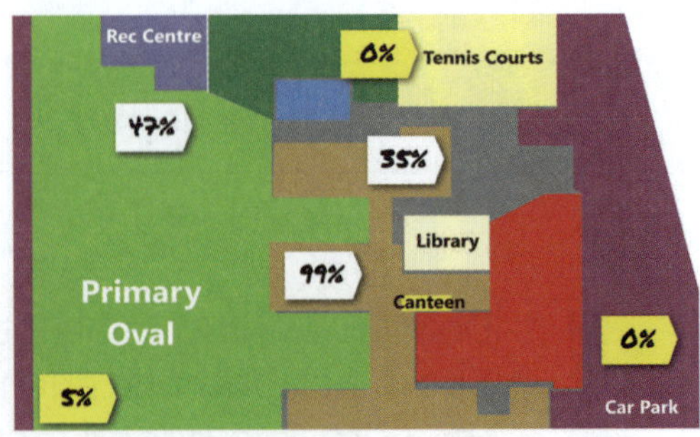

TARGETING STEM JOURNAL 5 @ PASCAL PRESS ISBN 978-1-925726-10-7

1 Record your measurements below.

Location	Signal strength %	Signal strength dBm

2 Mark the blind spots on the map. Ask your school's IT person where the Wi-fi hubs are in the school and mark those on the map as well.

3 Analyse your findings. Are there any important places (such as classes or admin areas) on your map that don't have Wi-fi? Use your measurements and the map to suggest where additional Wi-fi hubs could be located to cover the blind spots.

____

____

____

WI-FI SIGNAL STRENGTH METER APPS

Apps may request location permissions. Use the 'only while device is in use' settings for privacy.
Keep the device still for 30-60 seconds in each location for the best readings.
Suggested app for Android: Wifi Intensity
Suggested app for iOS:

DBM: MEASURING SIGNAL STRENGTH

Most signal strength meters will show signal strength as a percentage. The weaker the signal, the lower the percentage is. Most apps will also show the strength measured in decibel-milliwatts, or dBm. dBm values will most likely be negative, such as -30dbm. Values closer to 0dBm are stronger than those further away. -20dBm is quite strong. -90dBm is quite weak.

Binary beads

How can we code our initials as a string of beads?

Being electrical, computers can only work with data that has been stored as a series of 'ons' and 'offs'. In the binary code computers use, a 0 (zero) is off and a 1 (one) is on. Letters are stored as a code of eight 1's and 0's. For example, the letter T is 01010100.

What you need

different coloured beads

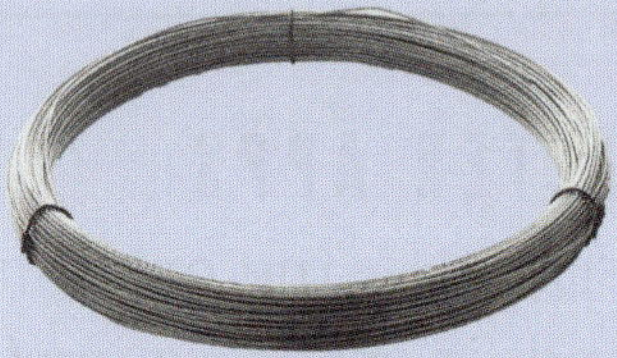
wire

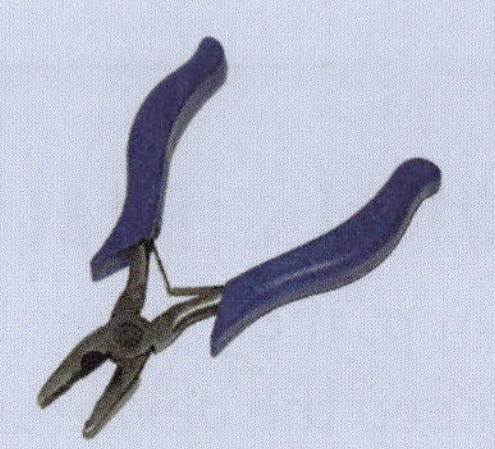
pliers

1 Complete Journal 1 and 2.

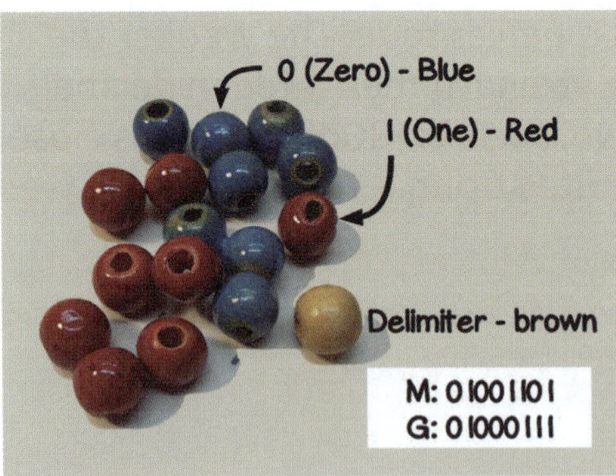

2 Use your guide from Journal 2 to thread the beads onto the wire. Don't forget the delimiter bead so that you can tell where one code ends and the next starts.

3 Bend the wire to prevent beads falling off.

4 Decide how to mark your binary bead string so you know where they start and finish.

TARGETING STEM JOURNAL 5 @ PASCAL PRESS ISBN 978-1-925726-10-7

1 Choose a colour to represent 0 (zero), a colour to represent 1 (one) and a 'delimiter' colour to separate the two patterns.

0 (zero) colour	1 (one) colour	Delimiter (gap) colour

2 **a.** Write your two initials in the circles below.

b. Look up the letters in the ASCII chart and write their 0's and 1's in the second row. The first three digits are the same for all the letters.

c. Colour in the squares beneath using your three chosen colours.

First letter:								Delimiter	Second letter:							
0	1	0							0	1	0					

3 Place the class's binary beads in one place. Select a bead chain to decode.

a. Copy the colours into the table.

b. Use the ASCII chart to decode the letters.

c. Match the initials to the student and check your answer.

First letter:								Delimiter	Second letter:							
0	1	0							0	1	0					

ASCII Chart

Letter	ASCII Code	Binary	Letter	ASCII Code	Binary
A	065	01000001	N	078	01001110
B	066	01000010	O	079	01001111
C	067	01000011	P	080	01010000
D	068	01000100	Q	081	01010001
E	069	01000101	R	082	01010010
F	070	01000110	S	083	01010011
G	071	01000111	T	084	01010100
H	072	01001000	U	085	01010101
I	073	01001001	V	086	01010110
J	074	01001010	W	087	01010111
K	075	01001011	X	088	01011000
L	076	01001100	Y	089	01011001
M	077	01001101	Z	090	01011010

41

Binary tower display

How can we use towers to convert a decimal number into binary?

In the decimal system, each column has ten times the amount of the one before. In the binary system, each column only has twice as much.

What you need

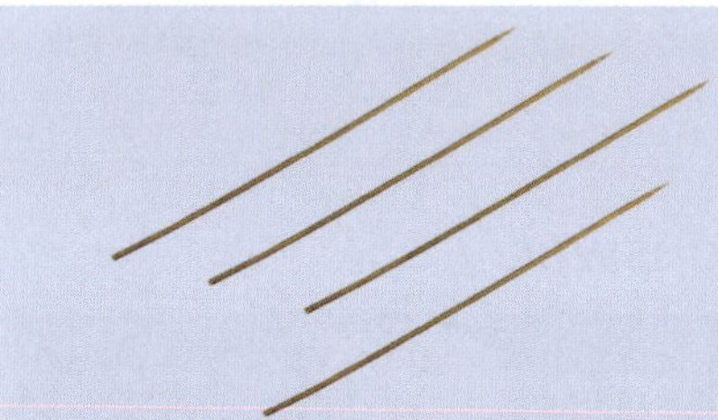
four skewers

corrugated card

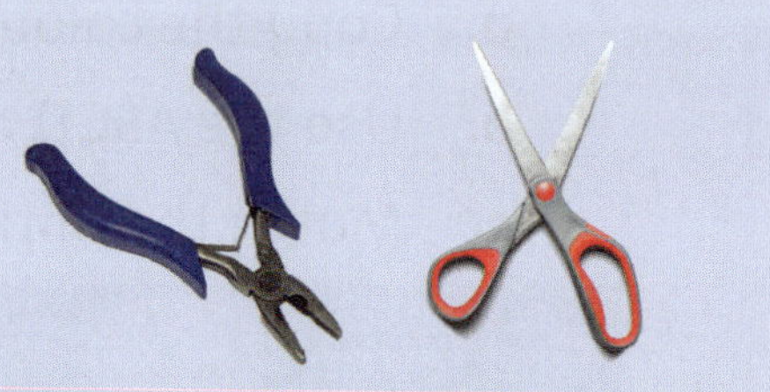
pliers, scissors

1 Cut your skewers to the lengths in the table in Journal 1.

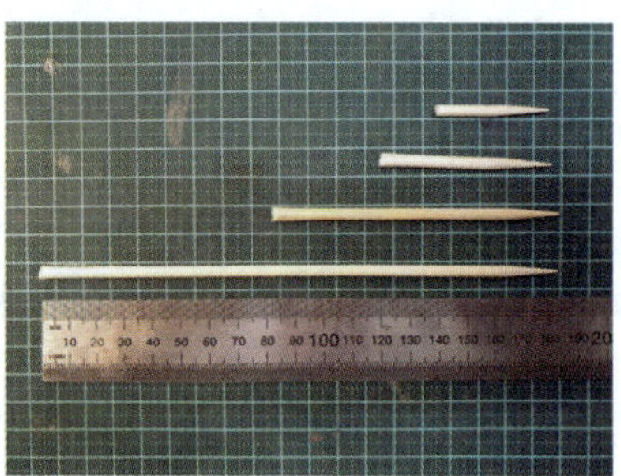

2 Cut out a 12cm × 3cm rectangle and two 8cm × 3cm rectangles.

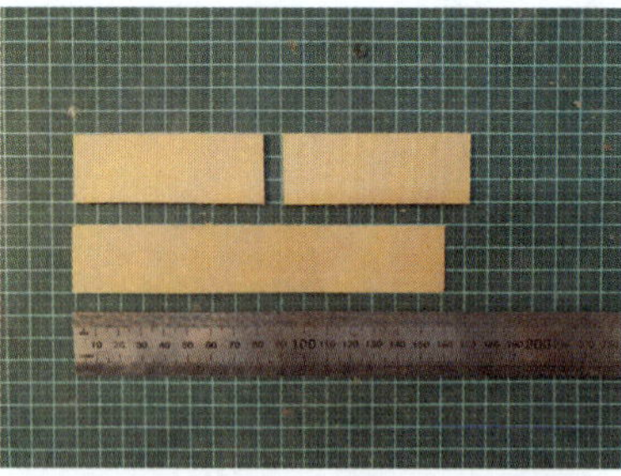

3 Push each skewer 2cm into the edge of the 12cm ×3cm card. Write the numbers 8, 4, 2 and 1 below each skewer.

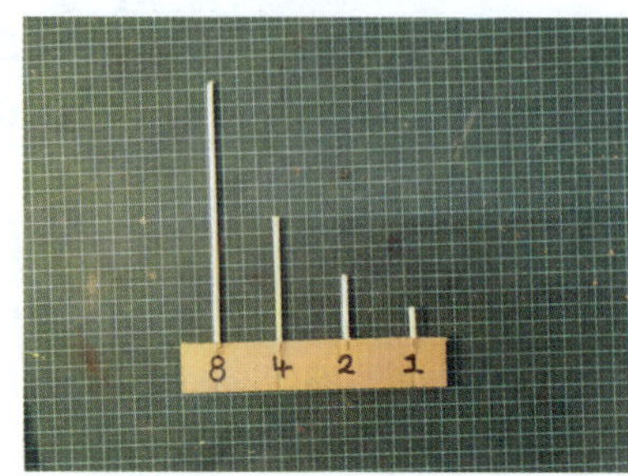

4 Hot glue the 8cm × 3cm supports to each end of the card so it can stand.

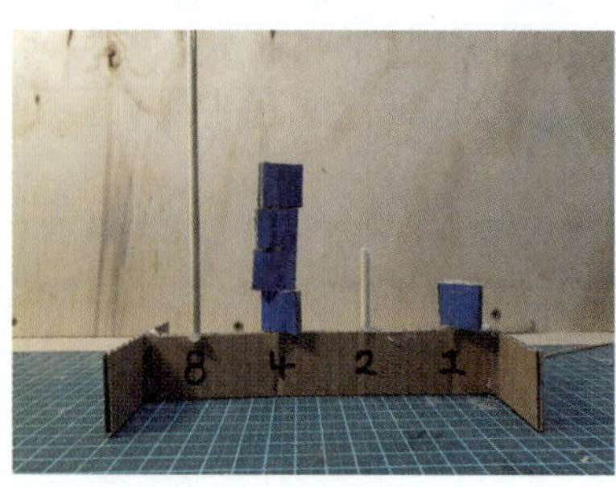

SCIENCE

MATHEMATICS

TARGETING STEM JOURNAL 5 @ PASCAL PRESS ISBN 978-1-925726-10-7

1 Use this table to measure and cut your labels. Mark 2cm from the pointy end of each one so you know how to far to push it in.

Skewer	Binary Label	Length
A	1	2cm + 2cm = 4cm
B	2	4cm + 2cm = 6cm
C	4	8cm + 2cm = 10cm
D	8	16cm + 2cm = 18cm

2 Cut out 5 squares of corrugated card. Each one should be 2cm × 2cm in size. Push a skewer through the edge of each one so they will slide onto the towers. (Note: This is definitely easier if you follow the direction of the corrugations!)

3 Use your towers to change '5' into a binary number. Procedure:

1. Start with the tallest tower that you can fill with squares.
2. Move onto the next tallest tower and repeat until you have no squares left.
3. Write the binary number: '0' for empty towers and '1' for full towers.

a. You have 5 squares. Which is the tallest tower you can fill completely? Fill the 4 tower.

b. You have 1 square left. Which is tallest tower you can fill? Fill the 1 tower.

c. Write down the binary number '1' for a full tower and '0' for an empty tower: 101

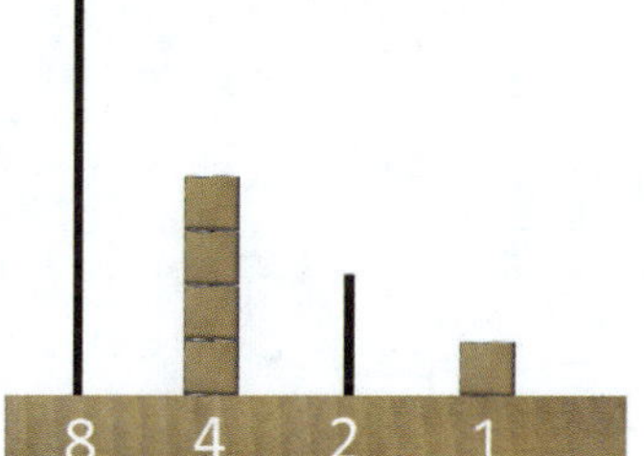

4 Use your tower to convert these numbers into binary:

a. 7 ______________________________

b. 6 ______________________________

c. 13 ______________________________

5 Convert these binary numbers back into decimal.

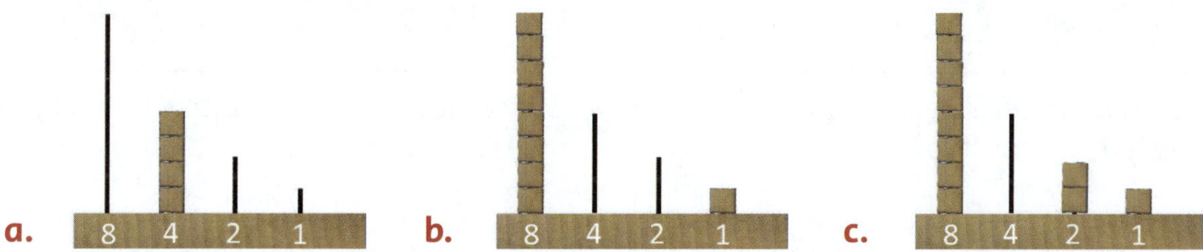

6 Adapt your binary towers to count numbers bigger than 15.

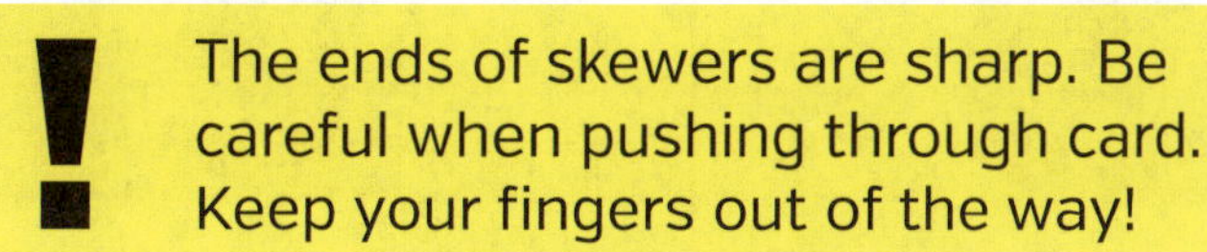

Decimal to binary

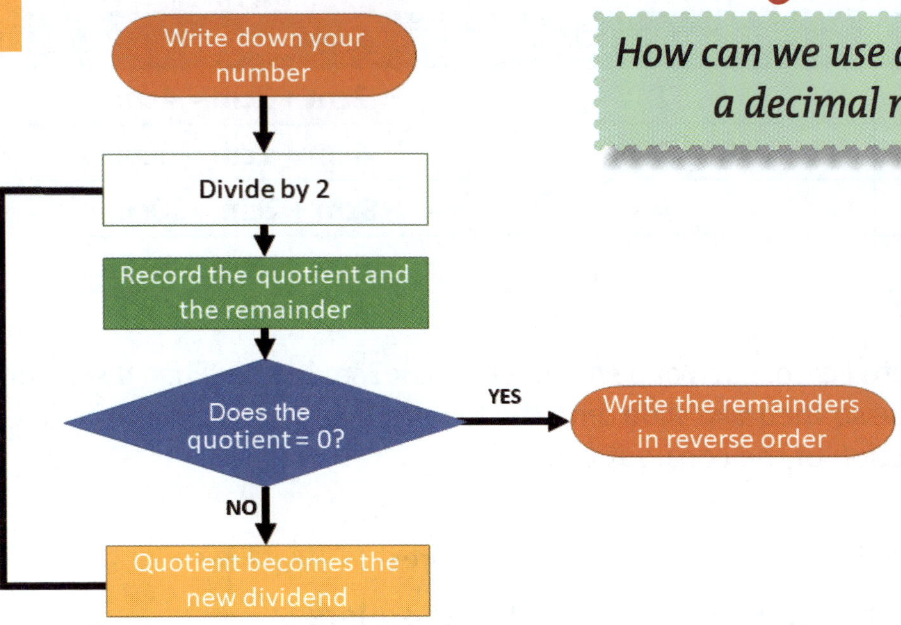

How can we use dividing by two to convert a decimal number into binary?

If you divide a number by 2, the remainder is always zero (for even numbers) and 1 (for odd numbers). This algorithm uses repeated division and remainders to convert a decimal number into a binary number.

What you need

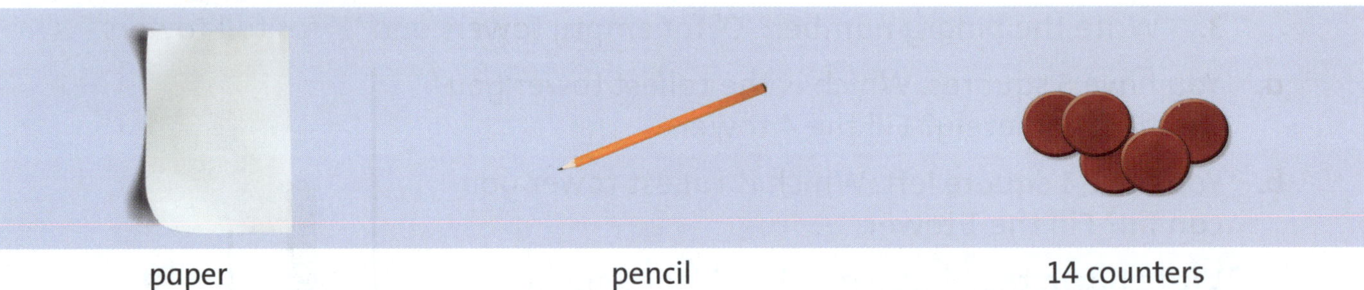

paper pencil 14 counters

1 Draw a four-square grid.

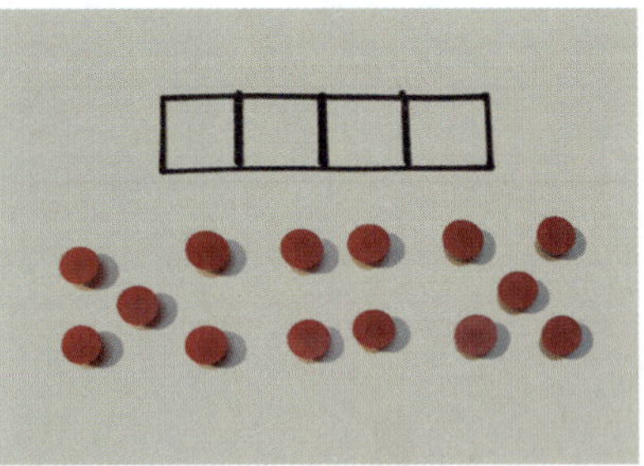

2 Divide your counters into two groups. Write the remainder in the last blank square.

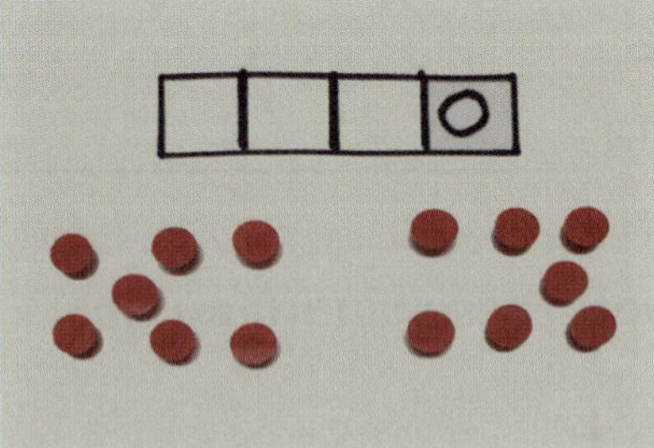

3 Put one group to the side. If you have any counters left, repeat step 2.

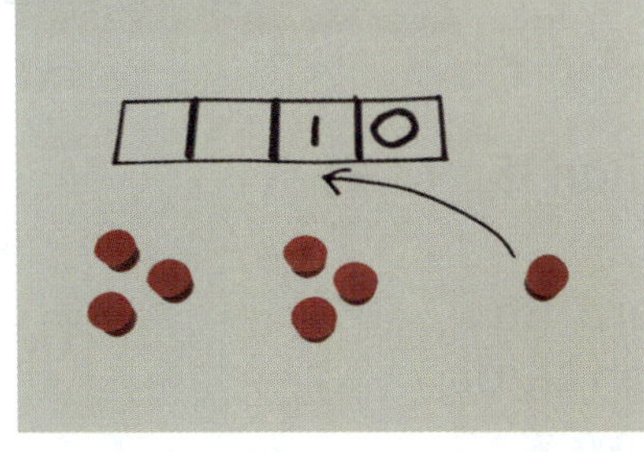

4 When you have no counters left, your grid will show the number in binary.

TARGETING STEM JOURNAL 5 @ PASCAL PRESS ISBN 978-1-925726-10-7

1 Here's the same process but written down. Use the example to convert 9 into binary.

a.

	Divisor	Quotient	Remainder
14	÷ 2 =	7	0
7	÷ 2 =	3	1
3	÷ 2 =	1	1
1	÷ 2 =	0	1

14 (decimal) is represented by 1110 in binary			
1	1	1	0

b.

	Divisor	Quotient	Remainder
9	÷ 2 =		
	÷ 2 =		
	÷ 2 =		
	÷ 2 =		

9 (decimal) is represented by _____ in binary			

2 Larger numbers will require more steps. Convert two numbers between 16 and 31.

a.

	Divisor	Quotient	Remainder
	÷ 2 =		
	÷ 2 =		
	÷ 2 =		
	÷ 2 =		

___ (decimal) is represented by ___ in binary			

b.

	Divisor	Quotient	Remainder
	÷ 2 =		
	÷ 2 =		
	÷ 2 =		
	÷ 2 =		

___ (decimal) is represented by ___ in binary			

Note: Answers are not supplied to open-ended questions where students' responses will vary.

1. Who lives Where? Page 3
3 Mediterranean Biome

3. Duck Adaptations 2 Page 7
1 The petroleum jelly waterproofs the card.
2 The conditioner adds a thin layer of oil to the feathers.
3 The oil comes from the preen gland.
4a It also removes the oil.
4b The birds would not be water resistant and could drown.

7. What's the Matter? Page 15
3c Sand is a solid as it has a definite shape and can be piled.

8. Frozen Cold Page 17
5 Salt is put on icy roads to lower the freezing point of the water on its surface so that it can't freeze.

9. Better Butter Page 19
3 The marbles speed up the churning.

10. Gas Power Page 21
2 Bubbles in the water.

11. Take the Pressure Down Page 23
1a The straw goes up.
1b The straw goes down.
3a Higher pressure outside the jar pressing down on the balloon.
3b Lower pressure outside the jar. The air inside presses up.
4 Top: straw, Bottom Left: Card, Bottom Right:jar.

12. Liquid Speed Bumps Page 25
3 Oobleck (magic mud), slime, chilled caramel topping, silly putty, plant resin, ketchup.

13. A Year's a Long Time Page 27
4b Jupiter's year is 12 times longer than ours.
4c Walking may not be half the speed of running, measurements not accurate

14. Happy birthdays to me Page 29
2a Earth
2b Mercury
2c Neptune
2d Mars
2e Jupiter
3b 340 birthdays
3c Uranus

17. Solar system stop-motion Page 35

Earth	12	11	10	9	8	7	6	5	4	3	2	1	12
Mars	12	11½	11	10½	10	9½	9	8½	8	7½	7	6½	6

Earth	12	11	10	9	8	7	6	5	4	3	2	1	12
Mars	6	5½	5	4½	4	3½	3	2½	1	1½	1	12½	12

2a When Mars is at 12
2b When Mars is at 6

Earth	12	11	10	9	8	7	6	5	4	3	2	1	12
Venus	12	1½	3	4½	6	7½	9	10½	12	1½	3	4½	6

TARGETING STEM JOURNAL 5 @ PASCAL PRESS ISBN 978-1-925726-10-7

18. Solar Cooker Page 37

4 The screen reflects sunlight in, the inside is dark to absorb light.

21. Camera Obscura Page 43

1a The scene upside down.
2 Top: light ray from head, pinhole, screen.
Bottom Light ray from feet, upside down image.

24. Magic Refracting Pencil Page 49

2a Closer
2b Deeper
2c Light rays change direction when they travel from water to air but our brains assume they have travelled in a straight line.

28. Night Into Day Page 57

4 Yes, as solar lights may not work if a bright light is shining on them.

32. Natural Dyes Page 65

2b Dyeing can happen at b (as fibres), c (as material) or d (after washing)

34. Dish-washer VS Dishwasher Page 69

4 Advantages for hand washing – safer for fragile pieces, more thorough at removing food.
Advantages for dishwashers – higher temperature, stronger chemicals used, cheaper for hotels or restaurants

36. Eating Utensils Page 73

2a Some of these foods aren't usually eaten with utensils.
2b Gravy, mashed potatoes, non-sticky rice (slippery food!)
2c Snack foods, food that needs slicing or cutting

38. Cable Treasure Hunt Page 77

1 Lightning (Apple iPhone, iPad to USB)
2 Display Port (computer to monitor / TV)
3 HDMI (Computer to monitor or TV)
4 3.5mm Audio (speakers / headphone to computer)
5 Ethernet (network to computer)
6 VGA (Computer to Monitor)

41. Binary Tower Page 83

4a 111
4b 110
4c 1101
5a 4
5b 9
5c 11

42. Decimal To Binary Page 85

1b 9 (decimal is represented by 1001 in binary.)

Targeting STEM Journal - Year 5

Copyright © 2021 Pascal Press
ISBN: 978-1-925726-10-7

Published by Pascal Press
PO Box 250
Glebe NSW 2037
www.pascalpress.com.au
contact@pascalpress.com.au

Author: Tim Tuck
Publisher: Lynn Dickinson
Typesetter: Stacey Grainger
Designer: Janice Bowles
Editor: Vaishali Batra
Series Consultant: Narinda Sandry

Printed in South Korea by Prinpia Co., Ltd.

Notes

Notes